"I'VE ALREADY GOT A 401(k) PLAN. WHY DO I NEED THIS BOOK?"

Millions of Americans have a 401(k) plan, but not everyone is equally skilled at managing and investing their money. Illustrated with graphs and charts and written in easy-to-understand language, this book shows you how to squeeze the maximum return out of your most valuable retirement benefit. Get answers to the most important questions about your 401(k):

- How can I calculate the costs of my retirement and the future value of my investment?
- How can I really get to know my plan—including the fine print?
- What is the best way to contribute to my 401(k) plan?
- Which investments should I choose?
- What do I do if the market goes down?
- What are the main drawbacks to participating in my plan?
- Is it smart to borrow against my account?
- How can I make sure that my 401(k) money is in trusted hands?

Other books in the
Money ® America's Financial Advisor series:

How to Retire Young and Rich

How to Start a Successful Home Business

Paying for Your Child's College Education

The Right Way to Invest in Mutual Funds

Dollar Pinching: A Consumer's Guide to Smart Spending

Car Shopping Made Easy

Starting Over: How to Change Careers or Start Your Own Business

*Your Dream Home: A Comprehensive Guide to
Buying a House, Condo, or Co-op*

401(k)
Take Charge
of Your Future

Eric Schurenberg

WARNER BOOKS

A Time Warner Company

A NOTE FROM THE PUBLISHER

This publication is designed to provide competent and reliable information regarding the subject matter covered. However, it is sold with the understanding that the author and publisher are not engaged in rendering legal, financial, or other professional advice. Laws and practices often vary from state to state and if legal or other expert assistance is required, the services of a professional should be sought. The author and publisher specifically disclaim any liability that is incurred from the use or application of the contents of this book.

Copyright © 1996 by MONEY magazine
All rights reserved.

Warner Books, Inc., 1271 Avenue of the Americas, New York, NY 10020
Visit our Web site at http: // warnerbooks.com

W A Time Warner Company

Printed in the United States of America
First Printing: February 1996
Reissued: January 1998
10 9 8 7 6 5 4 3 2 1

Library of Congress-in-Publication Data

Schurenberg, Eric.
    401(k) take charge of your future / Eric Schurenberg.
      p. cm.
    Includes index.
    ISBN 0-446-67492-3
    1. Finance, Personal. 2. 401(k) plans. I. Title.
HG179.S333 1996
332.024'01—dc20   95-31324
                                     CIP

Cover design by Bernadette Evangelist
Cover illustration by Peter Hoey
Book design by Giorgetta Bell McCree

To Judy and Emilie

ACKNOWLEDGMENTS

If this book succeeds in helping employees to better manage their 401(k) plans, it is entirely due to the dedicated benefits professionals and financial planners who have patiently guided me over the years, correcting my mistakes and pointing me toward the real issues. Among those who generously lent their time and expertise to this book are: Jim Rushin and Ray Maddock of Hewitt Associates; Pamela Scott of Kwasha Lipton; Paul Westbrook of Westbrook Advisers in Ridgewood, N.J.; David Bugen of Individual Asset Planning Corp. in Morristown, N.J.; Bob Bingham of Bingham, Osborn & Scarborough in San Francisco; and Larry Mylnechuk of the Stable Value Association. I also owe a special thanks to Al Schlachtmeyer, David Stuart, Shelley Parsons, and Jennyfer Guebert of Hewitt Associates, who have done as much as anyone in creation to help employees appreciate their 401(k)s and use them to their best advantage.

Thanks as well to my editor Rick Wolff of Warner Books for his encouragment and kind words; to Penelope Wang and Judy Feldman, who are **MONEY** magazine's best minds on the subject of 401(k)s; to Caryn Feinberg and Gwenn Kapner of **MONEY**, whose business acumen has helped spread *Managing Your Future*, **MONEY** magazine's 401(k) newsletter, to 900,000 employees; and to my other editorial colleagues at **MONEY**, who picked up the slack while I wrote this book.

CONTENTS

CONTENTS

INTRODUCTION

Most of us aren't accustomed to thinking of the U.S. Internal Revenue Code as a force for good. That's partly because our political process assures that the tax code at any particular moment has less to do with sound policy than with which lobbies currently have Congress's ear. It's also because of the tax code itself—all 4,000 pages and 5.6 million words of it. It is so horrifically complex that not even experts can foresee all the ripple effects of any new tax provision. Even so, out of this sea of code sections and letter rulings, corollaries and subparagraphs, occasionally something washes up that is of genuine benefit to America and her citizens.

One of those pearls is the 401(k) savings plan. For millions of Americans, including me, it is arguably the sturdiest lifeline to a future of financial security. To employees who approach their 401(k) with the proper blend of discipline, patience, and basic investing know-how, it offers a reliable way to build a nest egg worth hundreds of thousands of dollars—or considerably more. No other investment even comes close. And for our savings-starved economy, the 401(k) is a godsend. As of 1997 the plans had already invested 675 billion dollars of employee savings that might otherwise have been consumed. Without that kind of savings push, the nation will inevitably see its standard of living decline.

Considering how indispensable 401(k) plans have become, it is amazing how accidentally they came into being. Unlike Individual Retirement Accounts, say, which have vocal supporters in Washington, no congressman ever campaigned for the creation of 401(k) plans. No think tank ever dreamed them up. Instead, Internal Revenue Code Section 401(k)—the brief passage that spawned the plans—was quietly slipped into the code by the Revenue Act of 1978, mainly to clear up a dispute over the taxation of profit-sharing plans. The section says, basically, that an employee savings plan can include a cash or deferred arrangement as long as the plan is designed to benefit low-paid as well as high-paid employees, among a few other requirements. Cash or deferred arrangements (CODAs, in employee-benefits jargon) were deals in which employees had the choice of taking their profit-sharing bonuses in cash (and owing taxes on them that year) or putting them into their savings plans and postponing their tax bill.

It took a quiet, religious, 38-year-old pension consultant named R. Theodore Benna to see the promise buried in Section 401(k)'s technical details. Benna had two key insights: first, he recognized that nothing in the law forbade an employer from applying CODAs to regular salary rather than just bonuses. He also saw that companies could chip in extra money to the plan to encourage employees to save, thus helping to ensure that the plan would serve all employees. While Benna's inspiration complied with the letter of the law, it was so novel that no one could be sure it would win the approval of the Internal Revenue Service. As a test case, his company, Johnson Companies, set up a savings plan modeled on his idea. In November 1981 the IRS finally gave the design the green light.

Benna could not possibly have anticipated how his brain-child would flourish. According to estimates by Access Research, Inc., more than 26 million employees at some 210,000 companies are now eligible to participate in 401(k) plans. Three-quarters of those workers actually do take advantage of the opportunity, and many of them have already racked up impressive savings. The average active employee in a plan has more than $32,000 in his or her account. Nearly 20% of them have more than $50,000.

The projected growth of the plans is equally astonishing. By the end of the century, the amount of money invested in 401(k)s is expected to exceed a *trillion* dollars. Within 10 years the money stored in 401(k)s will be corporate employees' single largest source of wealth—exceeding not only the value of their other retirement plans, but also the equity in their homes.

Obviously, 401(k) plans could not have achieved such widespread acceptance had they not fitted conveniently into several themes sweeping corporate America. Most important, perhaps, is the reengineering of the U.S. corporation. To a cost-conscious corporate treasurer, 401(k)s are the perfect retirement benefit. Compared to traditional pensions, they are less expensive to administer (about $89 per employee in a small company, compared with as much as $500 for a pension) and easier for employees to understand and appreciate (which means the employer generates more goodwill for the buck with a 401(k)). Perhaps most important, 401(k)s absolve the employer of any responsibility to make sure that you take any specific amount of money with you when you retire. In a 401(k) plan, it's up to you—and you alone—to make sure you have enough money when you leave.

For employees, this aspect of 401(k)s requires a radical change in thinking. With a 401(k), the payoff you get from your company retirement plan depends first of all on you. If you don't take the initiative to contribute to the plan, it will do nothing for you at all. Unless you learn to invest it wisely, it will never live up to its potential. These are not small matters. As you can see from the chart on page xvi, postponing your first investment from age 25 to age 40 will shrink your returns by more than half. And if you think you can ignore the realities of investing your plan, look at the chart on page xvii. Choosing investments that underperform by as little as one percentage point a year can shrivel your nest egg by more than $150,000 over the course of your career. Make no mistake: Decisions you make (or avoid) today regarding your 401(k) have real consequences.

That's where this book comes in. It's intended to help you make the right decisions regarding your 401(k) at every point in the process—from enrollment and your first investment choices through finally withdrawing your money. While many employers make an effort to help their employees understand their plans, the educational materials they provide are often hopelessly superficial and vague. That's partly because companies have agendas they don't disclose to employees. For example, all companies worry tremendously about being sued if employees see them as giving advice that doesn't work out. Some companies want you to invest your 401(k) in the company's own stock, even if that's a bad idea (as it usually is). Whatever this book's shortcomings, pulled punches and hidden agendas won't be among them. As an objective guide unaffiliated with any 401(k) sponsor, this book's only agenda is to help you make the most of your 401(k).

The good news is, making the most of your 401(k) is not as difficult a task as you may think. Even if you're a complete novice at investing, you *can* master your 401(k) and take charge of your future. While some of the investing concepts you will encounter in the chapters ahead may be unfamiliar, they are not mysterious. The principles behind them obey all the laws of common sense. The fact is, you don't have to be a Wall Street wizard to earn a respectable return from your 401(k). All you need is a firm grasp of the basic investing principles outlined in this book and the combination of gumption and patience to abide by them.

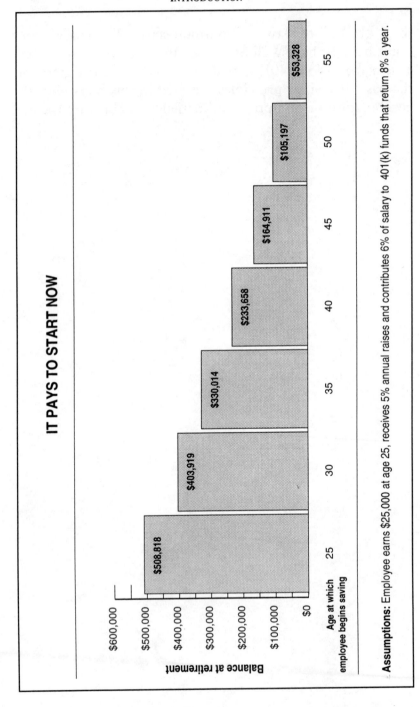

IT PAYS TO START NOW

Balance at retirement

$600,000
$500,000
$400,000
$300,000
$200,000
$100,000
$0

Age at which employee begins saving

25 — $508,818
30 — $403,919
35 — $330,014
40 — $233,658
45 — $164,911
50 — $105,197
55 — $53,328

Assumptions: Employee earns $25,000 at age 25, receives 5% annual raises and contributes 6% of salary to 401(k) funds that return 8% a year.

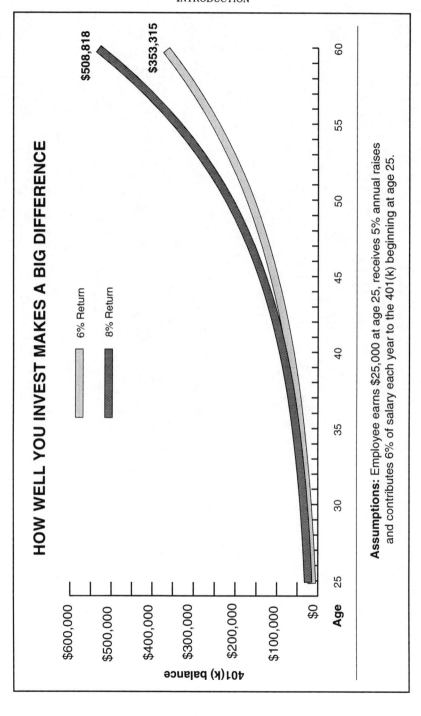

HOW WELL YOU INVEST MAKES A BIG DIFFERENCE

6% Return

8% Return

$508,818

$353,315

401(k) balance

$600,000

$500,000

$400,000

$300,000

$200,000

$100,000

$0

Age   25   30   35   40   45   50   55   60

Assumptions: Employee earns $25,000 at age 25, receives 5% annual raises and contributes 6% of salary each year to the 401(k) beginning at age 25.

CHAPTER 1

The Best Investment Around

Suppose a stockbroker called you and pitched an investment that he claimed would shave thousands off this year's tax bill, earn a guaranteed return of 25% to 100%—instantly—and not generate a penny of future income taxes until you decided to sell. If you were smart, you'd mutter something about calling the securities regulators and hang up.

Chances are, though, you've already been pitched this investment or something very like it—but by your employer, not by your stockbroker. The investment, of course, is your 401(k) plan. Your company may call it something different: the savings plan, capital accumulation plan, retirement program, or the like. But under any name it is one of the rarest creatures in the financial world: an investment that sounds too good to be true—and happens to be true anyway.

Strictly speaking, a 401(k) is an employee benefit, in that you can participate in one only if you're an eligible employee of a company that offers the plan. And like any other employee benefit, 401(k)s are subject to a maze of government regulations and specific rules imposed by your employer.

But it's misleading to think of your 401(k) as a perk like medical benefits or disability insurance that you get simply by showing up to work. It is an *investment*, and you have to manage it like one. After all, participation is completely optional. And the return you get from it depends entirely on how much money you put into it, and when, and how you apportion your money among the investment options you're given. In that respect it's not much different from investing in mutual funds through Merrill Lynch. In fact, you'd be perfectly justified to hand that money to Merrill Lynch instead of your 401(k) plan if you were convinced the brokerage's merchandise would earn you a higher return. But the fact is, it almost certainly can't.

There's nothing magic about the 401(k)'s investment superiority. In effect, Uncle Sam has fixed the fight—by imposing a drastically lighter tax burden on 401(k)s than on almost any other kind of investment. Your employer may get into the act as well, kicking some of its own money into your account for every dollar that you invest. That makes the 401(k) pretty hard to beat. (It's as if your stockbroker agreed to give you, say, $50 for every $100 you invested with him. That would be an irresistible investment, except that the broker would be out of business in about a week.)

Let's take a closer look at all the things that 401(k)s have to offer.

Your Contributions to the Plan Are Tax-Deferred

You're going to encounter the term **tax-deferred** throughout this book, so we should get it cleared up right away.

Tax-deferred means that you are allowed to put off paying federal income taxes (and state income taxes everywhere but Pennsylvania) on the money you save in the plan. The same friendly tax treatment also applies to any interest or other return that the plan generates. You eventually have to pay up when you withdraw money from the plan—the plans are tax-*deferred*, remember, not tax-*exempt*—but in the meantime, all of your savings can grow undisturbed by the IRS. Think of the 401(k) plan as a kind of temporary tax haven, a sort of Cayman Islands for your money. Everything that goes into the plan escapes the long arm of the U.S. tax collectors, as does everything that goes on within the plan. But once your money comes out, the revenuers will demand their share at last.

The fact that your contributions are tax-deferred means, in effect, that you get a tax write-off for every dollar you put into the plan. The process works by what the accountants call **salary reduction**—that is, every dollar you save in the plan reduces the taxable income you have to report to the IRS this year. Say, for example, that you earn $30,000 and you decide to contribute 6% of that amount (or $1,800) to your 401(k). When your W-2 arrives at the beginning of next year, it will show that your earnings subject to federal (and most state) taxes were $28,200. In other words, so as far as this year's tax bill is concerned, you never earned the salary that you routed into your 401(k).

Because you don't have to pay taxes on your savings, it takes less self-sacrifice to put money away in a 401(k) than in almost any other kind of investment. Say, for example, that you are in the 28% federal tax bracket and the 5% state tax bracket. (That means that of each additional dollar you earn, you have to pay 28¢ to Uncle Sam and 5¢ to your state's tax authorities.) If you contribute $1,800 a year to your 401(k), you reduce your federal income taxes by $504 and your state income taxes by $90. In other words, you have contributed $1,800 to your future financial security,

HOW 401(k)s TAKE THE PAIN OUT OF SAVING

	Saver	Nonsaver
Salary	$30,000	$30,000
401(k) Contribution	($1,800)	$0
Taxable Income	$28,200	$30,000
FICA	($2,295)	($2,295)
Federal Income Tax	($7,896)	($8,400)
State Income Tax	($1,410)	($1,500)
Take-Home Pay	$16,599	$17,805
What It Costs (in take-home pay) to Save $1,800 in the 401(k)		$1,206

but you denied yourself only $1,206 in spendable income today. (The table above will take you through the arithmetic.) Think of it as a 33%-off sale on your retirement savings.

Your Investment Grows Tax-Deferred

An even more impressive way to measure the benefits of tax deferral is to look at how fast your money grows in a 401(k) compared with a fully taxable (but otherwise identical) investment. Suppose, for example, that instead of shunting that $1,800 a year into your 401(k), you decided to receive it as salary and invest it in, say, a certificate of deposit from your bank earning 7%. By the time the $1,800 reaches you, unfortunately, there will be only $1,206 left. That's all that would remain after the federal and state tax

4

men were finished with your paycheck. But, gamely, you hand the money to your bank and wait for it to grow.

Each year the CD generates $84 in interest (7% of $1,206), which you plow back into the CD to make it grow faster. But that $84 is likewise subject to state and federal taxes; so after figuring in taxes, your CD investment leaves you ahead by only $56 ($84 minus 33%) a year.

Your 401(k), by contrast, doesn't get bogged down by taxes. In that plan, your full $1,800 goes to work for you immediately, and its investment earnings get plowed back into your account at full strength. The result: Even if your 401(k) earns the same 7% as the bank CD, it will grow to a much larger sum much sooner. How much larger? Take a look at the chart on page 6. Assuming that you are in the 33% combined federal and state tax bracket and able to save $1,800 a year for 30 years, you would end up with $170,000 in your 401(k) plan and just $76,000 in the fully taxable CD.

Your Employer May Match Your Contribution

If tax deferral supercharges the return on the investments in your 401(k), the company match switches on double afterburners. In a match, the employer promises to kick in a certain amount—typically between 25% and $1.50—for every dollar you contribute. That means, in effect, that you get an instant return of 25% to 150% on your money—a claim that no other legal investment can make. And talk about boosting your returns: adding a 50% employer match to the plan represented in the chart on page 6, for example, zooms the plan's final payout from $170,000 to more than $255,000.

Not every company matches its employees' contribu-

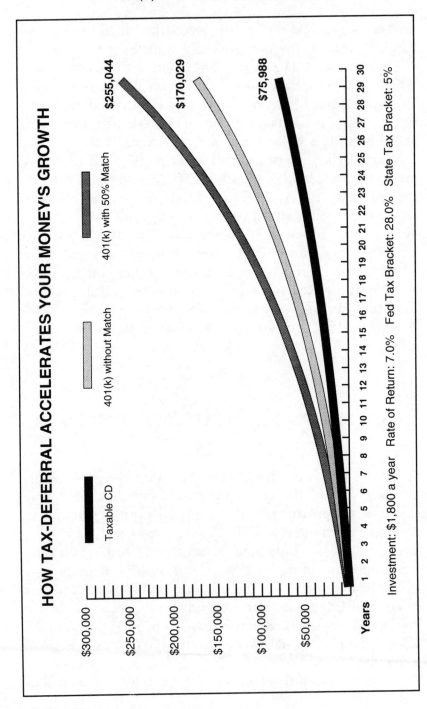

HOW TAX-DEFERRAL ACCELERATES YOUR MONEY'S GROWTH

Taxable CD

401(k) without Match

401(k) with 50% Match

$255,044

$170,029

$75,988

$300,000

$250,000

$200,000

$150,000

$100,000

$50,000

Years 1 2 3 4 5 6 7 8 9 10 11 12 13 14 15 16 17 18 19 20 21 22 23 24 25 26 27 28 29 30

Investment: $1,800 a year   Rate of Return: 7.0%   Fed Tax Bracket: 28.0%   State Tax Bracket: 5%

tions. Unlike tax deferral, the employer match is optional for plans that style themselves as 401(k)s. But the vast majority of companies do offer the option—about 84%, as of last count. And if your company is one of them, then your 401(k) plan is simply too compelling an offer to pass up.

You Save by Automatic Payroll Deduction

Whether or not to put money into your 401(k) is a onetime decision: once you sign up for the plan, your company automatically deducts your savings from each paycheck until you tell them to stop. This "autopilot" feature doesn't in itself improve your returns, but it removes one of the main psychological impediments to successful investing: human inertia. If every week or two (or however often you get your paycheck) you had to decide all over again whether to save, inevitably sometimes you wouldn't. One week the stock market might look too dangerous to you; another week you'd decide that you needed the cash for, say, your three-year-old's upcoming birthday party. Thus payroll deduction keeps you from talking yourself out of saving from time to time. Many employees, especially those making less than $35,000, say that automatic payroll deduction is the main reason they decided to invest in their 401(k).

The Plan Is Portable

Your 401(k) plan is designed and administered by your company (or by firms hired by your company), but once the money in your account is vested, it belongs to you.

(We'll talk about vesting in Chapter 3.) So if you leave your current job, you can take the money with you and roll it over into your new employer's 401(k) (assuming the new plan allows transfers) or put it into a personal tax-deferred savings account such as an Individual Retirement Account.

This eliminates the major drawback of the other leading kind of retirement benefit offered by many companies, the traditional pension. To earn a decent pension, you have to stick with one company for a long time. But how can you be sure you'll do that? By age 30 the typical worker has held 7.5 jobs. The way pensions are figured, the pension checks you'd earn in comparatively short stints with seven employers would barely add up to lunch money by the time you reach retirement. If you job-hop among employers with 401(k)s, however, your money hops with you, and your financial security barely misses a step.

There Is a Catch (of Course)

Uncle Sam has no interest in seeing today's employees become a financial burden on their fellow citizens in the future. That's why the government is willing to delay collecting tax revenue from 401(k) participants. (The actual "cost" of the 401(k) to the Treasury in postponed taxes is about $10 billion a year.) But in return, the government wants to make sure that the money put into 401(k)s really is saved for retirement. To do that, the tax code surrounds 401(k) plans with penalties that are triggered if you try to pull money out before you reach age 59½.

For starters, most companies flatly rule out withdrawals before your late fifties unless you leave your job, are disabled, or experience a financial hardship, which most plans define as needing the money to buy a house or avoid being evicted or foreclosed on in your current home, to pay for college, or to handle unreimbursed medical expenses. Whatever your excuse, if you take the money and don't roll it over into another retirement plan within 60 days, you'll owe full income taxes on the money withdrawn, plus a 10% tax penalty. That bites hard enough into your cash that a withdrawal generally doesn't make sense except as a last resort.

Most plans (about 75% of them) allow you to borrow against your account, within limits set by the government. Loans do allow you to get at your money without springing the tax traps laid for early withdrawals, but they have drawbacks of their own, which we'll discuss in Chapter 11. By and large, then, the best policy is to try not to get at your money before age 59½. Your 401(k), after all, was designed to be a retirement investment. Used that way—and managed according to the investing principles discussed in Chapter 5—it has no peer.

KEY POINTS

- Think of your 401(k) as an investment that you must actively manage.
- Because of the plan's generous tax treatment and the matching contribution from your employer (if your employer offers one), it's the best retirement investment you can find.
- The chief drawback to 401(k)s is that you have restricted access to your money until just before you reach retirement age.

CHAPTER 2

Why You Need a 401(k)

It has been barely two generations since many people started to be able to afford retirement—at least retirement as we think of it today, which basically means being independently wealthy by your early sixties. So many of the current generation of retirees have pulled it off, however, that it's easy to get too complacent. In a survey by one benefits consulting firm, three-quarters of today's workers said they were confident that they could retire comfortably. A Merrill Lynch survey found that most baby boomers expect to be able to say good-bye to the workplace by age 60.

Well, it may not be quite that easy. The generation that joined the workforce in the 1950s coasted into a comfortable old age on the strength of America's unparalleled economic dominance, an increasingly generous Social Security and corporate pension system, and housing prices that went through the roof. You will have to depend much more on your own wiles—and your own savings.

Think, for a moment, about what a financially independent retirement really means. It means that between your

Social Security and pension benefits (if any) and the income you get from your savings, you will be able support yourself, without working, at the same standard of living you enjoyed when you were at the peak of your career. That's a tall order. But it gets worse: you also have to be able to sustain that lifestyle for 25 or 30 years—or nearly as much time as you spent in the workforce—even as inflation grinds away at the strength of the dollars you've saved.

How much will it all cost? Without too much effort you can actually put an approximate price tag on 20 or 25 years of retirement. Working back from there, you can figure out how much you have to save, starting now, to build up that sum. This chapter will walk you through the assumptions you need to make about your future needs and the resources that will be available to you. You can then do the actual arithmetic using the worksheet on page 26. That worksheet will tell you, among other things, the sum that you need to have saved by the time you retire. Chances are you'll find that sum the most persuasive argument around for getting to work, right now, on making the most of your 401(k).

How Much Income You'll Need

Financial planners say that you can get by in retirement on between 70% and 90% of what you earned in your last year on the job without sacrificing your standard of living. Why less than your salary? Because many expenses drop away after you stop working. You won't have commuting costs, for example, or as much need for a dress-for-success wardrobe. Once you stop working, you also stop paying Social Security and Medicare taxes, which in 1998 sop up 7.65% of the first $68,400 of your income and 1.45% above that. Being relieved of these workplace expenditures is a bigger deal the lower your salary is. For example, if you make $30,000 and spend $100 a month getting to work, not having to commute cuts your cash outflow by 4% of your preretirement income. But if you make $100,000, retiring from commuting saves you just 1.2%.

As a result, the higher your salary, the higher your retirement income needs to be *as a percentage of your salary* to keep up your living standard. (Retirement planners call this crucial percentage the **replacement ratio**; you'll hear more about it later in this chapter.) Thus, if you make $40,000, you can figure on getting by on about 70% of the salary you earned in your last years on the job without missing a step. If you earn $250,000, you're going to need a replacement ratio of almost 90%. (For incomes in between, see the table on page 13.)

To the extent that people have focused on their retirement needs at all, they tend to underestimate them. According to a survey by the benefits consulting firm Towers Perrin, nearly two out of three employees making more than $50,000 thought that they'd need between 25% and 74% of their pre-retirement salary to avoid a decline in their standard of living. (Accountants put the correct replacement ratios at 71% and up.) Unless these workers are ready to spend their retirement in a grass hut, they may be in for an unpleasant surprise.

How Much That Income Will Need to Grow

An unpleasant surprise that awaits everyone in retirement is inflation. Even at relatively tame levels, it can still make a mess of your retirement plans. Consider: If prices rise by just 4% a year, the income that was comfortable when you were 60 would buy only two-thirds as much by the time you hit 70 and only half as much by age 78. When you're

HOW MUCH YOU WILL NEED
IN RETIREMENT

Salary before Retirement	Percent of Salary That It Will Take to Maintain the Same Standard of Living
$20,000	76%
25,000	73
30,000	72
40,000	71
50,000	72
60,000	72
70,000	75
80,000	80
90,000	83
150,000	86
200,000	87
250,000	89

Source: Alexander & Alexander Consulting Group, Georgia State University Center of Risk Management and Insurance Research.

working, you tend to cope automatically with creeping increases in consumer price, since your pay is likely to rise at least as quickly. Without a salary, though, there's only one way to protect yourself from inflation: go into retirement with plenty of savings in reserve.

How Long Your Money Will Have to Last

Life after work is stretching at both ends these days. Medical advances and a generally healthier population are pushing

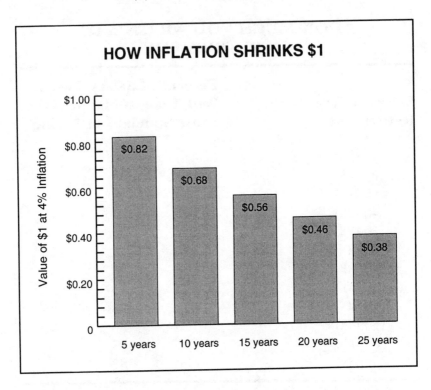

out the end of life, even as corporate downsizings are advancing the beginning of retirement.

For workers over 55, in particular, the opportunity to choose the moment of retirement is an increasingly rare luxury. Some employment experts say that if you're over 55 and work in a shrinking industry such as manufacturing or retailing, your chances of facing an early-out offer may be as high as one in four. While getting your walking papers from one job doesn't mean you have to stop earning income all together, your next job may not have the retirement benefits of your current one. All the more reason to load up your 401(k) while you can.

Your life expectancy is another target that may have moved since you last looked. You may have heard that the median life expectancy at birth is about 75. But that doesn't mean you should figure on just 10 more years once you hit retire-

HOW LONG YOUR MONEY
WILL HAVE TO LAST

Age	Men	Life Expectancy Women	Couples
55	22.3	27.0	34.4
60	18.5	22.6	29.7
62	17.1	21.2	27.8
65	15.1	18.9	25.0
67	13.8	17.4	23.2
70	12.0	15.3	20.6

Assumptions: Husband and wife are same age.
Sources: Society of Actuaries; Internal Revenue Service.

ment age. If you make it to age 65, statistics show, the odds are 50-50 that you'll make it to 81 if you're a man and 85 if you're a woman. If you and your spouse are both 65, there's an even-up shot that at least one of you will make it to 90.

Living too long or retiring too young are the quickest ways to break the bank during retirement. After all, if you planned for a 20-year retirement and end up spending 24 years after work, you'll need to come up with 20% more retirement income. That's why financial planners generally say you should lay away enough savings to get you into your early nineties at least—just in case you get lucky.

Where Your Retirement Money Will Come From: Social Security

Fortunately you don't have to rely on your savings for all the income in your retirement. For starters, Uncle Sam has promised to provide some help in the form of Social Security old age benefits. I know, I know: Uncle also promised to eradicate crime and put a chicken in every pot. It's clear to anyone who can add that Social Security will have to slash benefits for new retirees sometime before the avalanche of baby boomers starts to hit the system around 2010. The remaining workforce simply can't afford the taxes that would be required to uphold current benefits. But if you're old enough to be reading about 401(k), you probably will get *something* from Social Security, skeptical though you may be. How much you'll get depends a lot on how old you are now.

If you're over 50, your benefit will probably be pretty close to what the government now says it will be. No politician is suicidal enough to impose benefit cuts on people who don't have enough time to prepare for them. To find out what your benefits are likely to be, call the Social Security Administration at 800-772-1213 and ask for a Personal Earnings and Benefit Estimate Form. Mail it in and the feds will get back to you with an accounting of your past wages and an estimate of the benefits you will receive.

What you'll learn is that even if you're old enough to scoot in before benefits start being cut back, your Social Security check won't buy you more than a subsistence existence. The check you get is based on a mathematical formula that takes into account your average lifetime wages adjusted for inflation and your age at retirement. (Believe me, you don't want to know the details.) The calculation is set up so that the lower your wages, the higher your benefits as a percentage of your income. Thus, the replacement ratio is 42% if you've always earned average wages on Social Security's wage scale (about $23,000 today) and 26% if you've always earned the highest wage Social Security covers ($68,400 in 1998). So, at best, Uncle Sam will pay you a little over half of what you'll need in retirement if you're an average wage earner (a 42% replacement ratio when you need 71%). If you're a high wage earner, you'll get no more than a third (26% when you need 75%).

Remember, this is before the inevitable baby boom benefit cuts kick in sometime in the next century. **Money** magazine's estimate of the cuts that would be necessary to keep the system in the black suggest that if you're in your thirties, you should probably expect 25% less than Social Security now says it will give you. Kaycee Krysty, managing partner at the financial-planning firm Moss Adams in Seattle, plays it even safer. She tells her clients to save for retirement as if Social Security won't exist at all. That way whatever benefits do trickle in will be gravy.

But let's end on one kind word for Social Security. However meager the benefits may be, they have one major advantage. Once you start receiving them, they rise to keep pace with inflation. So if inflation runs 4% a year, your Social Security benefits will double in 16 years. They won't buy you any more than they did when you first started getting them. But they won't buy any less, either. That's more than you can say for some other popular sources of retirement income.

Where Else Your Retirement Income Will Come From: Your Pension

If you are fortunate enough to work for a company that offers a traditional pension as well as a 401(k), you have another potential source of income in retirement. You're more likely to have a pension if you work for a big company than a small one. Nearly nine out of 10 companies with more than 2,500 employees, for example, have a traditional pension, while only 45% of the companies with fewer than 100 offer them.

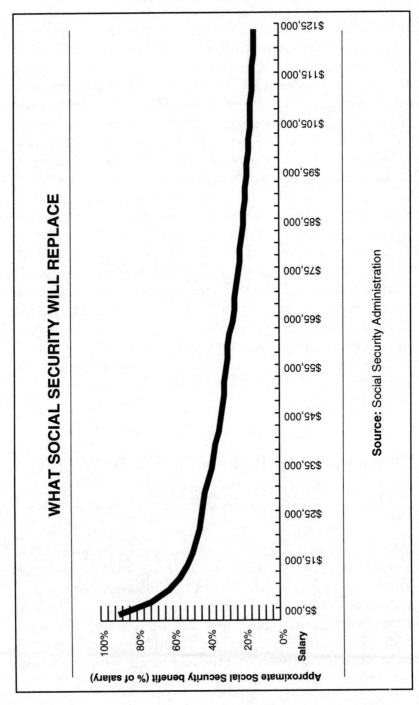

WHAT SOCIAL SECURITY WILL REPLACE

Approximate Social Security benefit (% of salary)

Source: Social Security Administration

Pensions are a throwback to the good old days of corporate paternalism. To collect a pension, all you have to do is put in time on the job. The company takes all the responsibility for saving and investing the money and making sure it's all there as promised when you retire. Once you leave work, the company then sends you a check once a month for the rest of your life. You don't have to worry about making sour investments or using up your money too soon—or much of anything except opening the monthly envelope.

There is one way you can blow it with a pension, however: You can change jobs. Pensions are designed to pay off most richly for workers who stay with a single employer for a whole career. It's all built into the formulas that companies use to decide how much of a pension you're entitled to. To simplify the formula a bit, a typical pension might promise to pay you a benefit equal to 1% of your last year's income times the number of years you served with the company.

So job-hopping penalizes you two ways: It lowers both the years of service and the salary level that will be worked into the formula. (Why? Because most people don't hit their peak earnings until just before they retire; so if you jump ship in midcareer, your pension from that employer will be based on that midlevel salary.) The result is that if you work 10 years each for three different employers, you're likely to get no more than about two-thirds of the pension benefits of one who toiled for a single employer for 30 years. It's enough to make you think three or four times before telling your boss to take this job and . . . well, you know.

There's another drawback to pensions: They leave you vulnerable to inflation when you're retired. While government pensions usually carry a cost-of-living adjustment, corporate pensions almost never do. It's too expensive. In the 1970s, when inflation was running at double-digit levels, companies often voluntarily gave their pensioners inflation boosts as a goodwill gesture. But in the past 10 years, only 44% have given cost-of-living raises, even though the cost of living rose 42% in the same period. The trend is scary: even if inflation isn't in the headlines every day, it can still eat away at a fixed pension check. Assuming inflation of just 4% a year, a pension check that covered, say, 25% of the income that you needed in the first year of your retirement would cover only 12% after 18 years.

The Gap

Even at its peak, Social Security wasn't designed to be more than a safety net, particularly for high-income earners. Nor were corporate pensions designed to do it alone, even for the relatively rare 30-year company veteran. The result: It's practically inevitable that your Social Security and pension benefit together will fall short of the income you need to keep up your standard of living in retirement. Generally, the higher your income and the shorter your final job tenure, the wider the gap will be. And just to keep things interesting, the gap you enter retirement with will inevitably widen over time, as your corporate pension check fails to keep pace with the inflation in your retirement income needs.

There's only one way to fill the gap: with the investment assets you've built up during your working life. If there were no such thing as inflation, you might aim to assemble a sum just large enough for the interest it earned to fill your retirement income gap. (And then you could leave the principal to your kids or donate it to your college and have a library named after you—or maybe a library carrel, depending.) But because inflation will widen the gap over time, you will need a considerably larger stash.

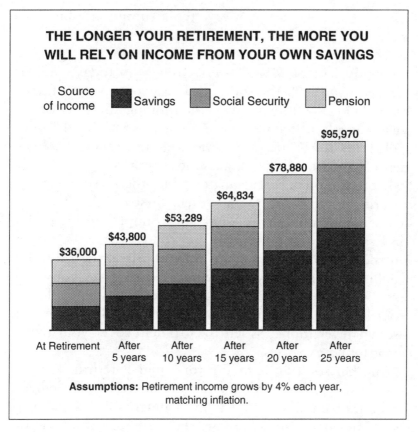

THE LONGER YOUR RETIREMENT, THE MORE YOU WILL RELY ON INCOME FROM YOUR OWN SAVINGS

Source of Income — ■ Savings ▨ Social Security ▢ Pension

$95,970

$78,880

$64,834

$53,289

$43,800

$36,000

At Retirement — After 5 years — After 10 years — After 15 years — After 20 years — After 25 years

Assumptions: Retirement income grows by 4% each year, matching inflation.

The exact size of this sum depends on a number of variables besides the size of your income gap. They include the rate of return you expect in retirement and how that relates to the rate of inflation, how young you plan to retire and how long you expect to live, plus the usual financial facts such as your tax bracket in retirement. The worksheet on page 26, for example, assumes that you will earn an after-tax return equal to three percentage points a year higher than inflation, about what you should expect in the long run from a conservative mix of stocks and bonds. For safety's sake, the worksheet also figures that you will live to 90 if you're male and 94 if you're female—or longer than about 85% of your contemporaries.

Granted, these are conservative assumptions, but they yield some truly eye-opening sums. If you expect to retire at 62, you should figure on reaching retirement age with the equivalent of $190,000 to $210,000 in today's dollars for every $10,000 that you need to generate out of your own savings. Different ways of running the calculations yield slightly different answers, but most are in the same ballpark. Clearly, if you're serious about financial independence, you are talking about serious money.

If these targets sound unattainable, there are two ways to bring them more within reach. First of all, you could lower your sights. You could, for example, decide to live on less income in retirement. Or you could decide to stay on the job longer. That not only shortens the time that you'll be relying on your savings, it also gives you some extra years to get the money together. Or you could sell your house when you retire, move to a smaller place, and use whatever money is left over to help cover your retirement living expenses.

Another solution is to aim for a higher return. Reason: If your investments throw off more interest in retirement, you can maintain the same living standard on a smaller nest egg. The effect can be striking. For example, if inflation is running 4% and you boost your rate of return from 7% to 9%, the nut you have to have saved up by retirement drops by about 20%.

Filling the Gap

The final line of the worksheet tells you how much of your salary you need to save each year to hit your retirement target. This is really the litmus test of whether your retirement goal is attainable or not. Here again, the amount of

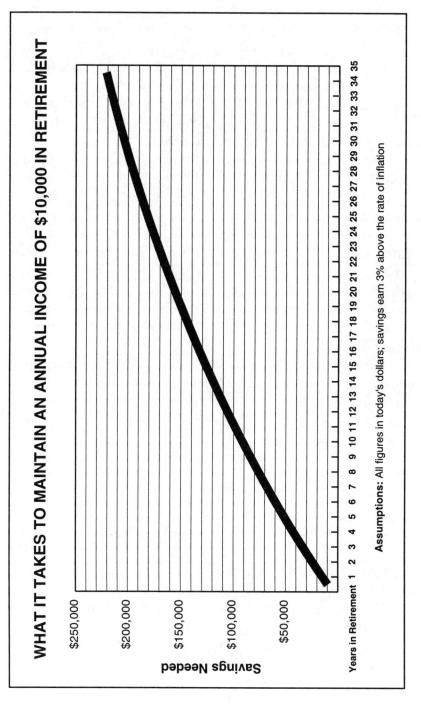

WHAT IT TAKES TO MAINTAIN AN ANNUAL INCOME OF $10,000 IN RETIREMENT

Savings Needed

$250,000

$200,000

$150,000

$100,000

$50,000

Years in Retirement 1 2 3 4 5 6 7 8 9 10 11 12 13 14 15 16 17 18 19 20 21 22 23 24 25 26 27 28 29 30 31 32 33 34 35

Assumptions: All figures in today's dollars; savings earn 3% above the rate of inflation time you have and the rate of return you get are the crucial variables. Assuming you earn a conservative 3% a year above the rate of inflation, you can put together a $200,000 retirement stash in 20 years by saving $7,400 a year. (Both figures are at 1998 dollars.) That wouldn't be easy for most people. But if you give yourself 30 years to reach your target, you'd only have to save $4,200 a year. In other words, by starting 10 years earlier, you could get by saving a little over half as much.

The other way to help bring retirement within your reach is to invest smarter. If you could earn 6% a year over the inflation rate—not a lay-up, by any means, but about the long-term average for the stock market—you could save a relatively bearable $5,400 a year for 20 years and still meet the $200,000 target. If you were able to earn 10% a year for the full 30 years, your $5,400 yearly savings would grow to about $430,000 in today's dollars—real retirement money.

That ought to suggest two principles that are absolutely fundamental to using your 401(k) to help you reach financial independence: Start early and aim for maximum return. Rest assured that you'll be hearing more about those principles in the pages ahead.

KEY POINTS

- Don't underestimate the cost of achieving a prosperous retirement. You probably won't be able to pull it off without saving religiously and investing intelligently.
- Social Security isn't going away, but it cannot help but get stingier, especially for workers now younger than 50.
- Your company pension can be an extremely generous benefit for long-term employees. But if you change

jobs frequently, you can't count on your pensions to add up to much.

- If you expect to reach financial independence in retirement, you are going to have to fund some of it out of your own savings. Almost certainly the price tag is going to run into the hundreds of thousands of dollars.

TAKE CHARGE OF YOUR FUTURE

	You	Sample (45–year–old married man, expects to retire at 65)
1. Current income	_____	$40,000
2. Annual income needed in retirement in 1998 dollars (70% to 90% of line 1)	_____	28,400 (71%)
3. Annual Social Security benefits (Call the Social Security Administration at 1-800-772-1213 for an estimate.)	_____	12,800
4. Annual pension benefits (Ask your employer for an estimate of your future pension benefits in today's dollars. For a ballpark estimate, multiply 1% of your salary by the number of years you expect to work for your company.)	_____	8,000
5. Retirement income from outside sources (line 3 plus line 4)	_____	20,800
6. Annual income needed from investments (line 2 minus line 5)	_____	7,600
7. Total nest egg needed (The savings needed to provide annual income equal to line 6 for the rest of your life. To calculate, multiply line 6 by multiplier A on page 27.)	_____	136,040

8. What you have saved already

_____ + _____ + _____ =

personal investments	vested amount in 401(k)	vested amount in other company savings plans		20,000

9. What your current investments will have grown to by the time you retire (line 8 times multiplier B on page 27)	_____	36,200

10. Additional retirement savings
needed (line 7 minus line 9)   99,840

11. Total annual savings still needed
(line 10 times multiplier C below)   3,694

12. Annual employer contributions to
your retirement plans, including 401(k)
match   800

13. Amount you need to set aside on
your own (line 11 minus line 12). $ 2,894

14. Percent of your salary that you need
to save each year (line 13 divided by
line 1)   7.2%

Age at which you expect to retire	Multiplier A		Years remaining until you plan to retire	Multiplier B	Multiplier C
	men	women			
55	22.1	23.5	1	1.03	1.0
56	21.8	23.2	2	1.06	.493
57	21.4	22.8	3	1.09	.324
58	21.0	22.5	4	1.12	.239
59	20.6	22.1	5	1.16	.188
60	20.2	21.8	7	1.23	.131
61	19.8	21.4	10	1.34	.087
62	19.3	21.0	12	1.42	.071
63	18.9	20.6	15	1.56	.054
64	18.4	20.2	18	1.70	.043
65	17.9	19.8	20	1.81	.037
66	17.4	19.3	25	2.09	.027
67	16.9	18.9	30	2.42	.021
68	16.4	18.4	35	2.81	.017
69	15.9	17.9	40	3.26	.013
70	15.3	17.4			

CHAPTER 3

Getting to Know
Your 401(k)

The sizzle in having a 401(k) comes from choosing investments and deciding how to allocate your money (and after that, of course, from watching the money add up). But you also have more than a passing interest in the guts of your plan: knowing where your money goes, who handles it, and what guarantee you have that it's being used the way you want it to be.

The best source of specific information about your plan is your benefits administrator, whether that title refers to one person at a desk in your company's human resources office or a field rep at the end of an 800 line in Cincinnati or Sioux Falls. There are some things, however, that your benefits administrator may not be able to tell you: for example, how your 401(k) compares with other plans or why the plan is set up the way it is. Also, like most 401(k) participants, you may have some questions about your plan's security against fraud and other financial mishaps. Answers to such questions—which, by the way, tend to be genuinely reassuring—may be more convincing coming from this book than from your employer.

How 401(k)s Evolve

Think of your 401(k) as a kind of three-way bargain involving the federal government, your employer, and you. All three parties share the goal of making your retirement more affordable, but they all also have their own particular interests to protect. The government wants 401(k)s to be broadly available, but it doesn't want to lose too much tax revenue in the process, so it sets limits on how much income employees can contribute. Likewise, your company wants the plan to be perceived as generous—especially in comparison with plans offered by rival employers—but at the same time, the company doesn't want to spend too much money or to overwhelm employees with too much choice. Balancing all this is your stake in the plan's design, which is simply that the plan be as generous as possible. To one degree or another, the tug-of-war among these interests shapes just about every element of your plan's design.

The Cast of Characters

The most prominent player in your 401(k) is the plan's **sponsor**, which is usually your employer. It's your company's responsibility to set the rules for participating in the plan, to choose the menu of investment options that the plan will offer, and to decide whether the plan will include optional features like hardship withdrawals, loans, or matching contributions. It's standard practice for companies to delegate much of the day-to-day administration of your plan to other firms, but the ultimate decision always rests with your company.

The law requires your company—and any other firm the company deputizes—to take its responsibilities toward your 401(k) very seriously. The people or companies that have decision-making power over any aspect of the plan are **fiduciaries**, a legal classification that basically means they must always act on behalf of the plan in an informed, prudent way. If they don't, they're held liable for any losses the plan suffers as a result of their missteps. Does that eliminate the possibility of fraud or negligence? Of course not. But it clearly helps. Where there have been misdeeds, they tend to occur in small-company plans where there are few people in a fiduciary capacity keeping an eye on each other.

As another safeguard, the assets of every tax-deferred retirement plan must be held in a trust to be administered solely for the benefit of the employees taking part in the plan. The trust is legally and financially separate from your company; that way if your employer runs into hard times, the corporate treasury can't, say, dip into the 401(k) to tide it over. The 401(k) is safe even if you or your employer goes bankrupt. Since the money is in a separate trust, creditors don't have any claim against it.

Like every other trust, your 401(k) has a **trustee**, who is responsible for collecting the plan's money, investing it, and then paying it out to retirees. The role may fall to an employee or committee of employees, though in larger plans the trustee is typically an institution, often the same one that manages the plan's investment funds. If so, the institution has the same fiduciary responsibility toward the plan and its participants as would the company's trustees.

While the trustees are responsible for seeing that the 401(k)'s money is well invested, they rarely actually decide which stocks and bonds the plan's funds should buy. Instead they delegate the day-to-day investment duties to one or more **money-management firms**. These can be firms you've never heard of that manage money strictly for retirement plans, or they can be household-name mutual fund companies, banks, insurers, or brokerage firms.

Employers also typically farm out the plan's bookkeeping tasks—tracking each employee's contributions and account balance, making sure that the plan complies with regulations, filing paperwork with the government and so on. This part of the job is known as **record keeping** or **administration**. Often a big financial-services firm like Fidelity or Bankers Trust will act as trustee, record keeper, and investment manager. In other cases, the money manager sticks to buying stocks and bonds and the record keeping is handled by a specialist like Hewitt Associates or Watson Wyatt Worldwide. Increasingly, the administrator's job description also includes creating communications programs that introduce employees to their plan and help them understand the basics of investing. In a 401(k), in which success depends on intelligent decisions by employees, education is increasingly becoming a crucial part of the package.

Getting Your Foot in the Door

Most companies require you to put in some time in the saddle before you can sign up for the 401(k). But as long as you're over 21, that waiting period can't be longer than a year.

Your employer can keep you on hold a touch longer, though, when it comes to **vesting**, the process by which you become legally entitled to the money in your account. Any money that you put into the plan remains yours, of

THE 20 BIGGEST 401(k) MONEY MANAGERS

Rank	Money Manager	% of All Large 401(k) Plans
1	Fidelity Institutional Retirement Services Co.	16.1%
2	The Vanguard Group	8.0
3	Cigna Retirement & Investment Services	3.1
4	Wells Fargo Defined Contribution Trust	3.0
5	Bankers Trust Co.	3.0
6	T. Rowe Price Associates	2.8
7	American Express Trust Co.	2.7
8	Merrill Lynch	2.5
9	The Principal Financial Group	2.4
10	State Street Bank & Trust	1.7
11	The Putnam Cos.	1.5
12	Massachusetts Mutual Life Insurance Co.	1.5
13	Smith Barney, Inc.	1.4
14	Invesco Funds Group	1.4
15	Twentieth Century Funds	1.3
16	Aetna Life Insurance Co.	1.3
17	Norwest Bank	1.2
18	Frank Russell Trust Co.	1.2
19	Mellon Bank	1.1
20	Metropolitan Life Insurance	1.1

Source: Judy Diamond Associates, Inc.

course, but in about 70% of plans you have to wait before you can lay claim to employer contributions. If that's the case with your plan, you'll face one of several vesting op-

WHEN YOUR EMPLOYER'S CONTRIBUTION BECOMES YOURS

Years of Service	Least Generous "Cliff Vesting" Allowed (% Vested)	Least Generous "Graded Vesting" Allowed (% Vested)
1	0	0
2	0	0
3	0	20
4	0	40
5	100	60
6	100	80
7	100	100

tions. You may, for example, have to work for the company for five years before you can be vested in any of your employer's contributions. At that point you vest all at once, a process known as **cliff vesting** in benefits jargon. More often, the plan will vest you gradually between your third and seventh year, 20% at a time. However your company chooses to do it, the law says you must be fully vested once you've worked for the company seven years.

How Much You Can Put In

Your employer sets the rules here, with one eye on staying competitive with other employers and the other eye on a maze of government regulations that decide which employees can contribute what. A typical plan might let you contribute between 1% and 15% of your salary as tax-deferred savings, known as **pretax** savings (because the money goes into the plan before income taxes are withheld). Less than half of all 401(k)s allow you to put in non-tax-deferred, or **after-tax** savings, as well. After-tax savings don't reduce your taxable salary when you make them, but once your money is in the plan, it is allowed to grow tax-free until you withdraw the money.

But when it comes to contribution limits, what you see in your employer's 401(k) brochures isn't always what you get. Depending on factors that are sometimes impossible to determine ahead of time, your contribution targets may be overruled by government regulations. Result: You may find that you can't put as much money into the plan as you expected. You may even have some savings returned to you, along with the investment earnings and matching contributions they'd accumulated. Or, depending on how your company chooses to handle it, you may find your pretax savings magically transformed to after-tax status.

The simplest of the government limits is a $10,000 maximum that the tax code imposes on tax-deferred employee contributions. This ceiling rises with inflation, but only if inflation has been steep enough to raise the price by more than $500 from the previous level. (So at a 3% annual inflation rate, the ceiling will rise every two years or so.) Chances are you won't have much problem with this limit. After all, if your company sets a maximum contribution of 15%, you'd have to earn more than $66,000 to come close to a $10,000 contribution.

Moreover, once you get much above that salary level, you get tangled up in a government restriction that may reduce your maximum contribution to just 5% or 6% anyway. The origin is a hideously complicated regulation designed to keep 401(k)s from being tilted in favor of what the tax code refers to as "highly compensated employees."

Simply put, the average percentage of salary that the highly paid put into the plan cannot greatly exceed the percentage that the rest of the staff put into the plan. If it looks as if that will happen in any year, the plan can require the highly paid to cut back their contributions. If the plan's administrator doesn't catch the problem in advance, it may even have to give the excess back to the high-income employees. That money then becomes part of their taxable salary for the year, which can be an unpleasant surprise.

Don't dismiss this as a problem strictly for the corner-office crowd. In the eyes of the law, anyone who is among the best-paid 20% of the staff and makes more than $80,000 (adjusted for inflation) is highly compensated. (Try telling that to a family straining to live on $80,000 in, say, San Francisco or New York.) As many as one in four 401(k) plans were tripped up by this **antidiscrimination rule**, as it is called, and the percentage will probably only go higher in the future.

Your benefits administrator can tell you whether the tax code counts you as one of the highly compensated. If so, ask whether the plan is in danger of flunking the antidiscrimination test. If the company has to refund some of your contributions, chances are it will do so by March 15 of the following year. (If the company takes more than 2½ months beyond its fiscal year to refund excess contributions, it faces a fine.) In other words, you could get a check representing a fat supplement to last year's income just as you are getting ready to file your taxes. The moral: If you're in the highly compensated club and your plan is in hot water with the antidiscrimination test, don't file your taxes until after the ides of March.

There's one more way you might be surprised by a limit on your 401(k) contributions. In an attempt to make sure that people don't shelter too much income from taxes, the IRS has ruled that you and your employer together can't contribute more than 25% of your salary (or $30,000, whichever is less) to all of your tax-favored retirement savings plans together. You are most likely to run into this problem if you're a big 401(k) saver (both pretax and after-tax contributions count) and you take advantage of other pretax benefits such as a dependent-care savings account. (This is a benefit that lets you put aside pretax money to cover day care expenses for children or dependent adults in your family.) Once again, you don't have to be rich to run into trouble: the employees most vulnerable are those with salaries around $30,000. Luckily, tax law changes will make this problem far less common beginning in 1998.

How Much Your Employer Can Put In

Here's where you find out just how generous your 401(k) is. More than 80% of companies with 401(k)s match employees' savings, but their magnanimity varies. About one in four kick in a relatively miserly 25 cents for every dollar that you invest. (Even so, that's the same as getting a 25% return instantly, which isn't peanuts.) Another 18% of employers match you dollar for dollar, and a very obliging 2% pitch in more than you do.

Now, not every plan matches every dollar you put in; often the match applies only to the first 3% or 6% you contribute. Also, your company may choose to make its contribution only in the form of company stock. But these are quibbles. However your plan matches your savings, it amounts to a gift from your employer. You shouldn't pass it up.

Why do companies make matching contributions? For the same reason they pay their employees: They want to attract and hold the most talented workers they can. They also want to help those workers go on to a prosperous retirement—not only because that's the responsible thing to do, but also because happy retirees make for good public relations.

There's also a more cynical explanation, if you prefer to look for such things. Because of the antidiscrimination rules, highly paid employees (including those responsible for designing the 401(k) plan) have an incentive to attract as many lower-paid employees as possible into the plan. Unless they get enough of their staff into the plan, they can't contribute as much as they'd like themselves. Generous matches are among the most reliable ways to get the attention of lower-paid employees.

Where You Can Put Your Money

One of the key features of 401(k) plans is the degree of flexibility they give you in investing your money. About 93% of employers give you at least three investment options—the average is 6—and the trend has definitely been to add options. (Only one in 50 companies limits employees to just one investment.) According to a survey by benefits consulting firm Foster Higgins, some 55% of companies have added investment options in the past two years. Just 1% have subtracted any.

Except for your employer's stock, almost all your choices in a typical plan are investment **funds** rather than direct investments in stocks or bonds. (The only exception: if your 401(k) is set up as a self-directed account with a brokerage. In that case you may have more or less free run of the investments the brokerage offers, including individual stocks and bonds.) In a fund, investors' contributions are collected under the direction of a professional money manager who uses the money to buy stocks and bonds on behalf of the fund. Your account is credited with **shares** or **units** that represent your proportionate ownership of the stocks and bonds in the portfolio.

The funds may be fairly small pools of money operated by investment firms that cater only to retirement plans. They may also be the same mutual funds that fund companies or stockbrokers sell to the public. Fidelity Magellan, for example, is one of the most popular choices both inside and outside 401(k) plans. More than half of the fund's massive $60 billion in assets represents contributions from 401(k) investors.

If your plan is well designed, each fund offered will follow a different investment approach, allowing you to mix and match your options to suit your investment needs. It's up to each fund manager to stick to the philosophy described in your plan's documentation. That way, when you put money into the stock fund, say, you know the fund will remain invested mainly in stocks, rather than bonds, money-markets, cattle futures, McDonald's franchises, or some other investment that may have caught the manager's fancy.

While half a dozen investment choices may seem like too many to keep straight, investment advisers say that five to nine funds gives you the proper range of choices without too much overlap between them. At the very least, your plan should include one choice from each of the three columns in the table on page 39.

We'll define these different investment options and discuss how they fit into your 401(k) investment strategy in later chapters.

When Your Money Is Counted

Considering how much of your money will be tied up in your 401(k), it's only natural that you would want to check

TYPICAL 401(k) INVESTMENT OPTIONS

Capital Preservation Funds (most conservative)	% offering	Bond Funds (conservative)	% offering	Stock Funds (riskiest)	% offering
Stable value (GIC) fund	79	General bond	29	Equity index	63
Money-market	48	U.S. government	20	Balanced	61
		Bond index	10	Growth/aggressive growth	54
				Equity-income	42
				International	23
				Life cycle	2

Source: Buck Consultants.

39

HOW OFTEN PLANS ALLOW YOU
TO SHIFT MONEY

Frequency of Transfers	% of Plans
Annual	3%
Semiannual	8%
Quarterly	42%
Monthly	12%
Daily	33%

Source: Foster Higgins.

on how it's doing. In most plans, the answer you get will be as of the end of the previous month or quarter. But more and more companies are updating the information daily. Today about two in three 401(k)s values accounts daily, compared with fewer than one in five four years ago. Benefits experts say that they expect almost all plans to switch to the speedier system within a few years.

Daily valuation has advantages beyond simply providing more timely satisfaction of your curiosity. Most of the plans that offer daily valuation permit you to switch your money among funds in the plan any day you choose, rather than on just four designated days a year (which is still the most common arrangement). So if you feel you can't stand another moment's risk in your plan's aggressive growth fund, for example, you can pull the plug immediately and move into a safer fund. As you will see in later chapters, it's not a good idea to shift your money around frequently—it's too easy to zig when markets are zagging. But having the ability to move at a moment's notice can actually make it easier to tough out a rough patch in the market. Some employers have found that their employees are more likely to lose their cool and change their account when they know they can make such adjustments only once every three months.

When You Can Take Your Money Out

The government—through its enforcers in the IRS—strongly encourages 401(k) investors to keep their money locked up in the plan until retirement. Uncle Sam nevertheless grants your employer the option of letting workers get at their money before retirement—subject to a few pounds of regulation, naturally. But if your company offers those early exit options in its 401(k), they give you considerable flexibility.

The best way to take money out of your plan while staying on the job is with a loan. And since you have to pay a loan back into your account, taking one out doesn't leave a permanent gaping hole in your 401(k). (We'll discuss the pros and cons of loans in more detail in Chapter 11.)

If your plan includes loans—as some three-quarters of plans do—the company must abide by another set of IRS regulations, which limit how much you can take out and how soon you have to pay it back. The company does have some discretion to set the interest rate it will charge you to borrow your own money, but the rate must be in line with prevailing loan rates. A plan might charge one or two percentage points above the prime rate, a benchmark interest rate used by banks in setting corporate loans. Depending on the plan's policy, the interest rate may be fixed at the time you take out the loan or it may fluctuate with prevailing interest rates in the economy.

Your plan may also offer a so-called hardship withdrawal

provision, which allows you to take money out of the plan before age 59½ without having to pay it back. However, you have to use the money for one of the following purposes: to pay college costs for yourself or a dependent; to buy a primary residence; to pay unreimbursed medical expenses; to prevent foreclosure on, or eviction from, your home.

The employer has to satisfy itself (and the IRS) that it isn't handing out money to phony hardship cases. So your company may ask you to prove that you couldn't get the money from any source other than a 401(k) withdrawal. If your employer prefers not to ask nosy questions about your finances, it is allowed to choose another alternative that is presumed to prove you're a true hardship case: it can suspend your 401(k) contributions for a full year after the withdrawal. Or it may give you your pick of the two alternatives and let you decide which works best for you. Either way, though, don't expect much sympathy from the IRS. You still owe full income taxes plus the 10% tax surcharge on the money you take out—despite the hardship.

You Know You Have a Top-Shelf Plan If . . .

- you can save up to 15% of your salary pretax.
- your employer kicks in 67 cents or more for every dollar that you contribute, up to 6% or more of your salary.
- the plan lets you transfer money between funds daily.
- you have at least half a dozen investment options.
- you are allowed to withdraw money before age 59½ for hardship withdrawals.
- you can borrow from your account.

Where to Learn about Your Plan and Your Account

Most employers provide much more information than they have to about managing and investing their 401(k). But that's not saying much. The law requires employers to provide participants with only three basic documents. The other communications that your company may well shower on you, from newsletters to retirement-planning software, are all voluntary—and not cheap. (But don't get too grateful just yet; there's a chance that you're paying for much of it out of your investment accounts.)

The basic documents that every 401(k) participant is supposed to see:

• *The Summary Plan Description (SPD).* A booklet that describes the plan, the SPD is a handy source for information on your plan's rules for eligibility, vesting, withdrawal rules, and so on. Like most legal documents, it can be rather dull and forbidding in appearance, though the law requires it to be written in plain English. Of course, plain English may not mean to you exactly what it means to the lawyers and actuaries who draft the SPD.

• *The Summary Annual Report.* An abbreviated version of the report that your employer has to file with the IRS, it focuses on the cash flows and assets of the plan as a whole. It can give a regulator an idea of your plan's overall performance, but there is little there that is likely to interest you. You can recycle it as soon as you get it.

• *Personal benefits statements.* Coming out quarterly at most companies, these statements contain critical information: how your funds have performed, how your money is allocated among the plan's investment options, and how much you and your employer have contributed to the plan.

When you get yours, check it to make sure your plan's allocations are still close to what you intended. (Things could have changed if, say, the stock market had a rally and your non-stock funds did not.) You should also double-check for mistakes: Make sure that the opening balance matches the closing balance on your previous statement; that your contributions have been recorded correctly; and that any changes you made in your investment allocations were picked up.

If your company wants to provide more information about your investments, you're also likely to encounter the following materials:

• *Mutual fund prospectuses.* If your plan uses mutual funds for its investment choices, you will probably be handed these legal documents, which generally make the SPD seem like beach reading. Fortunately most of the useful information about the fund pops up in the first three or four pages: the explanation of the fund's investment approach, fees, and past performance. (We'll go into these in more detail in Chapters 6 and 7.) The Securities and Exchange Commission (SEC) has been allowing some fund managers to test shorter, simpler prospectuses. If the abbreviated materials work—meaning if the SEC decides that they hit all the high points despite their brevity—it could become much less tedious to get the information you need about your funds.

• *Interactive voice response systems.* About 35% of 401(k) plans already offer this service, and another 19% say they plan to start using one in the next year or so. That's a fine development if you don't mind conducting your 401(k) business by tapping numbers into a touch-tone phone rather than talking to a person (although a live operator is an option in about three-quarters of the plans). These systems can be convenient, allowing you to check on your account balance and make transfers 24 hours a day. But remember, even with the automated systems, transfers aren't necessarily instantaneous. Trading requests can't always be executed the day you place them (if you make them on weekends, for example), and on high-call-volume days you may not be able to get through to the system at all.

• *Newsletters, brochures, meetings, audio/visual presentations.* These are among the other methods companies use to communicate information about the benefits of your 401(k) plan and basic investing concepts. The quality can vary widely, but even if your employer's communications are among the best, there's one important—and deliberate—omission. They won't tell you specifically how to invest your money. Your benefits department, after all, is not in the investment management business. Besides, employers are extremely leery about crossing the line that separates dispensing information from giving advice. The fear: The advice may not pan out and the employer could be sued.

The bottom line: It's much easier than it used to be to get information about your plan and its investment choices. But the most crucial decisions in managing your plan— how much to put in it and where to put it—remain your responsibility alone.

Who Pays

The average cost of administering a 401(k) ranges from some $89 a year per participant for plans with fewer than 100 employees down to $45 or so for plans with more than 1,000. On top of that are the investment management fees, which run from 0.2% of the money invested to about 1.5%, depending on the kind of fund (stock funds are pricier than bond funds) and whether it's a private investment fund or a mutual fund (mutual funds cost more).

Generally speaking, the employer pays the operating expenses and you pay the money-management fees (which are deducted automatically from your account). Unfortunately, more companies are pushing the administrative expenses onto the employee. For example, in 1988 only 11% of employers made their employees pay record-keeping fees; by 1995 that had risen to 63%. Your summary plan description might spell out who pays what in your plan; if not, ask your benefits administrator.

All else being equal, the lower your expenses the better, since whatever comes out of your account detracts from your return. That's especially true when the fees are charged as a percentage of your assets, as is the case with investment management fees. As a fiduciary, your employer has a responsibility to make sure that the managers it hires charge reasonable fees. (Chapter 7 will tell you how to find out the fees that your fund charges.) But it's also up to you to keep those charges in mind when you choose funds for your account. If the charges seem too high, let your plan administrator know that you're not happy about it.

KEY POINTS

- The people with authority over your plan are fiduciaries, which means they are legally obligated to make sure the plan is run solely for the employees' benefit.
- For further safekeeping, the plan's assets are kept in a trust that is legally and financially separate from your company.
- Every plan is subject to complicated government rules that may limit the sum you can put into the plan. You need to be particularly conscious of these restrictions if you make more than $66,000.

- If your employer matches your savings with contributions of its own, take advantage of it.
- Other optional features to hope for: plentiful investment options, daily valuation, hardship withdrawals, and loans.

CHAPTER 4

Decision Number One

After you've been with your company for a year or so, you will be invited to make your first decision regarding your 401(k). Do you want to enroll, and if so, how much do you want to contribute? If you've read this far, the recommended answer should be obvious. But in case you skipped the first three chapters: The answer is yes, definitely yes, as soon as you can for as much as you can afford. The 401(k) is a great investment vehicle, but like the vehicle in your garage, it won't take you anywhere unless you turn the key. Unfortunately, saving money is one of those things, like cleaning out the basement or going to the gym, that are easy to decide to do and even easier to decide to do later. It requires a certain leap of faith to resist splurging on something you want today in the interest of a goal that is decades in the future. Even if you accept the need to save, you still have to weigh whether retirement is really the most pressing savings goal you have right now. And not least, you have to find a way to come up with the money. All in all, these and other obstacles keep one of every four workers eligible for 401(k) from contributing to one. You should resist making the same mistake.

The Case for Investing

As Chapter 2 made clear, your income from Social Security and your pension simply won't cover what you need to maintain your standard of living in retirement. You could resolve to work indefinitely, but that's the sort of idea that sounds much better at age 30 or 40 than at 60 or 65. (It says something about the popularity of working indefinitely that only about 15% of people 65 and older work today, a figure that has fallen steadily from 22% in 1974.) By the time you hit your sixth decade, your health and stamina will probably not be what they once were, and you may simply be tired of your job and ready for a change. Remember, too, that these days it's increasingly likely that you won't get to choose the age at which you retire. Your employer may take the decision out of your hands by laying you off. Forced retirement in your fifties or sixties—an age when you may not necessarily be a hot commodity in the eyes of potential employers—is much easier to face with a healthy stash in your 401(k).

The Case for Starting Now

There are three ingredients to building a solid retirement fund: the money you put into it; the rate of return you get; and time. You've seen how the 401(k)'s tax advantages, not to mention the company match, allow you to put more money to work at a higher rate of return than in virtually any other investment. The time element, though, is entirely up to you.

It's impossible to overemphasize the importance of getting an early start. As your money starts to grow, the interest your money earns starts to earn interest itself. This snowballing effect is known as **compounding**. Given time, it acquires a momentum that Albert Einstein (no stranger to large numbers himself) once called "the eighth wonder of the world."

Here's how it works. If you save $1,000 a year and earn 8%, your investment earns $80 the first year. Nothing to get excited about. But once you've built your stash up to $12,500 (which would take 10 years at 8%), the interest on your savings will add more each year to your 401(k) than your own contributions. By 15 years from the starting point, your annual investment earnings will more than double your annual contributions, and by 20 years out, they will more than triple them. In effect, your money will be working three times as hard as you. The higher your returns, the more powerful the effect of compounding. If you earn 10% on your investments, for example, the annual interest you earn will overtake your annual contributions within eight years and double them within 12.

HOW LONG IT TAKES BEFORE
ANNUAL INVESTMENT EARNINGS SURPASS
ANNUAL SAVINGS

Rate of Return	6%	7%	8%	9%	10%
Years until Annual Return Overtakes Annual Contributions	12	10	9	8	7

The real penalty for putting off investing in your 401(k) isn't so much the contributions you fail to make, but the missed opportunity to let that money grow 10 or 15 years down the road. Take a look at the chart on page 52, for example, which shows how two employees would fare, both contributing $2,000 a year for 25 years to their plan but starting at age 25 and 35, respectively. (Let's assume they earn 8% on their investments.) Both save a total of $50,000 over their careers, but by age 60 they wind up with wildly different sums. The early starter finishes with more than $315,000, the late starter with less than half as much ($146,000). The early starter's advantage is due entirely to the extra 10 years of compounding. In fact, the early starter could have stopped contributing the same year that the late starter began—and would still have come out far ahead by age 60 with $198,000 (see the chart on page 53). In other words, he could have saved only 40% as much as the late starter and still come out with 35% more money. No wonder Einstein was impressed.

The Only Good Reason to Wait

Important as it is to start building your 401(k) as soon as possible, retirement isn't your only savings goal. Buying a home and sending your kids to college are two major saving targets that you will have to work toward at the same time. But there's one matter you should take care of before you lock up money for any of these long-term purposes. You need to assemble enough readily available money to see you through any emergency that may crop up. That way, if you fall ill, your furnace blows, or—God forbid—you get laid off, you can see yourself through without having to raid your 401(k) or any other long-term stash.

Your emergency reserve should equal three to six months' living expenses. That's living expenses, not salary:

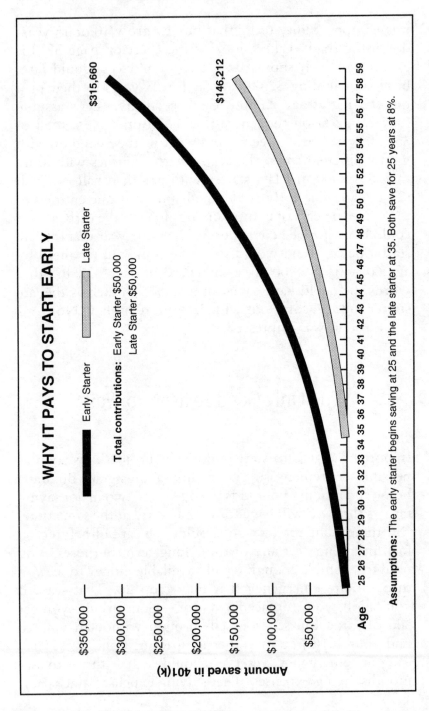

WHY IT PAYS TO START EARLY

Early Starter   Late Starter

Total contributions: Early Starter $50,000
                          Late Starter $50,000

$315,660

$146,212

Amount saved in 401(k)

$350,000
$300,000
$250,000
$200,000
$150,000
$100,000
$50,000

Age 25 26 27 28 29 30 31 32 33 34 35 36 37 38 39 40 41 42 43 44 45 46 47 48 49 50 51 52 53 54 55 56 57 58 59

Assumptions: The early starter begins saving at 25 and the late starter at 35. Both save for 25 years at 8%.

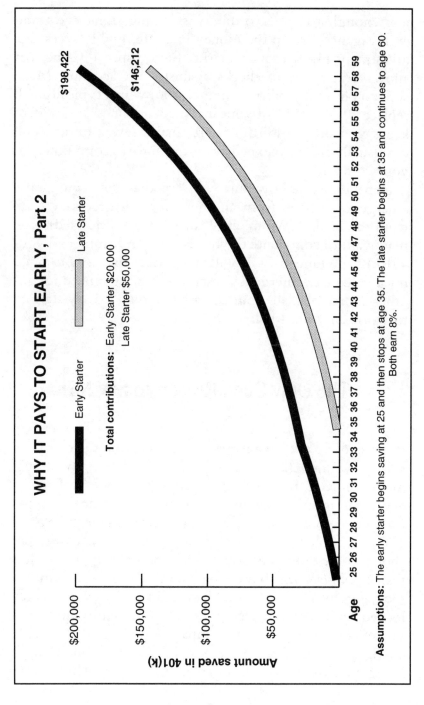

WHY IT PAYS TO START EARLY, Part 2

Early Starter

Late Starter

Total contributions: Early Starter $20,000
Late Starter $50,000

$198,422

$146,212

Age 25 26 27 28 29 30 31 32 33 34 35 36 37 38 39 40 41 42 43 44 45 46 47 48 49 50 51 52 53 54 55 56 57 58 59

Amount saved in 401(k)

$200,000
$150,000
$100,000
$50,000

Assumptions: The early starter begins saving at 25 and then stops at age 35. The late starter begins at 35 and continues to age 60. Both earn 8%.

just enough to cover ordinary spending, sans taxes and extravagances. Keep the money in a safe, highly accessible investment like a money-market fund, especially one that allows you to write checks against your account. Make sure you have disability insurance, too, which typically will replace 60% to 65% of your income if an illness or accident keeps you off the job for more than a few months. You can usually buy it inexpensively through a group policy at your company.

Depending on how sure you are that you could raise emergency money from another source if necessary (say, from the bank of Mom and Dad or rich Uncle Ned), you may want to contribute to your contingency fund and your 401(k) simultaneously. It will take longer that way to build up an adequate emergency reserve—hence the need for another source of cash—but at least you won't delay starting to work on your 401(k).

The Only Good Reason to Say No

Because of its tax advantages (not to mention the company match), your 401(k) is virtually always your best investment for retirement. But virtually always isn't always. There is one circumstance in which the 401(k) might not be superior—if its investment options are clearly inadequate.

That's probably the case if your plan's only investment choice is the company stock. This situation applies to less than 1% of 401(k)s, but it's one to avoid. The problem: It's too dangerous to have more than about 10% of your money locked up in your employer's stock. No matter how optimistic you are about your company's future, keeping your 401(k) solely in company stock links your financial well-being too closely to the health of one company. The security

of your job and your pension already depends on the sound-
ness of your employer. There's no need to add your 401(k)
nest egg to the same basket.

Even if the sole choice is not your company stock, a
401(k) with only one investment offering is less than ideal.
Still, any other investment that might crop up in a one-
choice plan, most likely a conservative insurance company
contract, at least won't steepen your exposure to the fate
of your employer. You might consider contributing to such
a plan, especially if it comes with a match. But check it out
carefully. (We'll discuss what to look for in typical 401(k)
investments in later chapters.) And to spread your risks
around, make sure that you own dissimilar investments
outside your 401(k).

Not a Good Reason to Say No

Some investors challenge the wisdom of investing in a
401(k) because there's a chance that taxes may go up in the
future. Better to pay taxes at today's rate, goes this argument, than to defer them now and face what may be a
higher rate when you pull your money out of the account
in the future. Nonsense.

For one thing, there's no point at all in trying to map
your finances in anticipation of tax rates in the distant future.
It's difficult enough to predict tax brackets from one con-
gressional election to the next, let alone one decade to the
next. In the past 10 years, for example, the top tax bracket
has changed five times. It is not the sort of speculation on
which you should base your long-term investment planning.

Besides, it's not necessary for your tax bracket to be lower
in the future for a 401(k) to improve your returns. The real

power of tax-deferred investing comes from allowing your money to compound without having to pay a toll each year to the IRS. After 20 years of tax-deferred saving in a 401(k), you'd still be ahead of a taxable investment even if Congress hoisted your tax rate from 28% to 44% the day you retired. (And that assumes you take none of the elementary tax-cutting steps described in Chapter 12 to protect your 401(k) payout; so in reality, your tax bracket would have to rise much higher than 44% in retirement to wipe out the head start you get from the 401(k).) The difference is even more pronounced if the company offers a match. If your employer kicked in 50% of what you saved, your tax bracket would have to rise from 28% now to 63% in retirement to wipe out the benefits of 401(k) investing. Say what you like, no politician is greedy enough to raise middle-income taxes *that* high.

How Much to Put In

The argument for putting as much money as you can into your 401(k) is just as convincing as the argument for getting an early start. It's simply a numbers game. If you increase your contribution by 25% and keep it up, you'll raise your eventual payout by 25%. That can add up to a tidy sum, given enough time. For example, $100 a month invested at 10% starting at age 30 works out to $325,000 by the time you're 65. Raising the ante to $125 a month increases your retirement sum by 25% to more than $406,000. A company match only emphasizes the advantages of saving more. If your company kicked in 50 cents for every dollar you contributed, then your 401(k) stash in the above example would jump to $610,000—all from contributing $125 a month.

Of course, when you reach the point on the enrollment

form where you actually decide how much of your salary to devote to your 401(k), it ceases to be a game. Every percentage point of income that you shunt into your 401(k) represents money that can't be used for other investment goals, such as your kids' college fund, or for other worthy purposes, such as the rent or car payments or safari vacations in Tanzania. Setting your contribution level is a balancing act, in which you have to weigh the plentiful good your 401(k) will do for you in the long run with other, more immediate needs for your money.

The purist approach to this dilemma is to figure out exactly what you need to save each year to meet each of your financial goals in the future—and then save that amount, using your 401(k) for the bulk of your retirement savings. If you like this approach, a professional financial planner can help you do the arithmetic and help you choose the investments to create the plan. If you prefer to make your own money management decisions, you may get all the number crunching you need to create a plan by logging onto one of the several websites that feature retirement planning calculators. Among those worth visiting are Quicken.com (www.quicken. excite.com) and **MONEY** magazine's site (www.money.com).

The alternative approach is more seat-of-the-pants: Make an effort to save 10% to 15% of your income in your twenties and thirties and 15% to 20% in your forties and fifties. Then start allocating your savings among your goals.

Financial planners generally recommend that your 401(k) should get at least as much as your employer will match—typically 3% to 6% of your salary. Failing to claim every dollar of your company's contribution is the moral equivalent of not cashing part of your paycheck. And you can't go back and claim an employer match later by making larger contributions when you can afford them better. Once your paycheck is printed, so is the chance to make a matched contribution for that pay period.

In addition to the portion of your salary that is matched, most companies will let you save another 4% to 9% of your income on a pretax, unmatched basis. That's your best bet if you want to sock away additional retirement savings.

The one exception: If you think you may need the money within a few years, you might consider *after*-tax contributions instead, if your company is one of the minority that offers them.

There are trade-offs to be made regardless of whether you choose pretax or after-tax contributions. With pretax savings your money goes farther because you can put the whole sum to work without sharing any of it with Uncle Sam. But your access to that money is strictly limited. After-tax contributions, by contrast, lack the extra kick of an up-front tax deferral, but you can withdraw the money at any time without penalty. You'll owe taxes only on the portion of the withdrawal that represents your investment earnings.

Pretax savings are less painful to make if your plan offers loans or hardship withdrawals, since that means your money isn't *completely* locked up. You don't have to pay taxes on the money you borrow from your plan, but the loan amount is limited to half your balance or $50,000, whichever is less—and you have to pay back the money. Hardship withdrawals, in turn, don't have to be paid back, but you can make them only for specific purposes. Worse, you have to pay full taxes on whatever money you withdraw, plus the 10% early withdrawal penalty if you make the withdrawal before age 59½. (For more on getting at your money before retirement, see Chapter 11.)

The bottom line: Don't contribute to your 401(k) at all unless you're planning to save that money for retirement. If your financial situation is reasonably stable and you think it unlikely that any unforeseen expense would overwhelm your emergency reserve or other assets, stick with pretax contributions. If not, if you don't feel comfortable subjecting your funds to the pretax withdrawal rules, try to talk yourself into it anyway. (Be sure to mention the possibility of borrowing and the emergency exit offered by hardship withdrawals.) But if your financial situation is so unpredictable that you just can't abide pretax savings, then go with the after-tax option. It's better than not saving for retirement at all.

Where to Find the Money

Because your contributions are deducted automatically from your pay, funding your 401(k) is a relatively painless way to save. You don't have to write a check every time you make a contribution, and you'll probably find that you don't even notice the missing income. The hard part is convincing yourself that you can afford to make the savings in the first place. According to a survey by the benefits firm Towers Perrin, employees who don't contribute to a 401(k) cite difficulty in coming up with the money as their number one excuse. (32% of noncontributors hid behind that justification. In second place, at 24%, were people who said they could get a better return elsewhere—a dubious assertion.) Here are some tactics that may make it easier to participate in your plan—or to increase your rate of contribution, if you're already on board.

• *The tough love approach.* The tactic starts with a stern self-lecture about the necessity to stop spending so much and start becoming financially self-sufficient. You then proceed to the fiscal equivalent of taking your medicine like a grown-up: you draw up a budget.

To do that, block out an hour or two to go through your checkbook register, credit-card statements, and receipts and see where your money is really going. You'll find that some of your costs are nonnegotiable, such as mortgage payments and taxes. Others are more flexible, such as food, utilities, and entertainment. Look for ways to cut those expenses by

5% to 10%. Exactly how to do that is beyond the scope of this book, but you'll find no shortage of smart shopping ideas on bookstore shelves or magazine racks and in conversation around the kitchen table with your aunt Sophie. If you really want to sink your teeth into economizing, pick up *Dollar Pinching: A Consumer's Guide to Smart Spending* by Shelly Branch (Warner Books; $10.99), which helps you save large sums of money on your biggest-ticket expenditures.

• *The frugality by theorem approach.* You may find that your biggest hurdle is convincing yourself that it's honestly worth skipping one ski vacation a year, say, to free up money to save for retirement. If so, remember the mathematical argument in favor of investing in your 401(k)—which is that your money is worth almost three times more to you if you save it in a matched 401(k) than if you spend it. The chart on page 61 shows why. For example, if you spend a dollar of your wages, you get only 56 cents worth of goods; the rest is intercepted by federal and state income taxes and sales taxes. But if you put that dollar in a 401(k), you save the whole dollar. And if your employer matches you 50 cents on the dollar, every buck you save buys you $1.50 worth of retirement investments.

• *Share your next raise with your 401(k).* How hard would it be to dedicate your next raise to your 401(k)? You know that you can live adequately on the salary that would be left, since you've been doing it ever since your last raise. Besides, you may find that you're not really giving up much extra spending money. For example, if you earn $45,000 and are in the 28% federal and 5% state tax bracket, a 4% raise gives you $24 more to spend each week. Harkening back to the frugality theorem, you'll get a lot more out of the raise if you put it into your 401(k) as a pretax contribution. Instead of $24 a week of extra spending money—or $1,248 over the entire year—you would add $1,800 to your annual 401(k) contributions. Assuming you earn 8% a year for 20 years, sacrificing that $24 a week will increase your

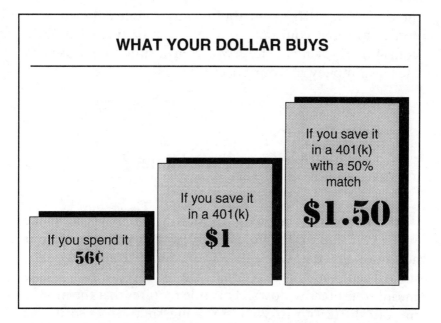

retirement fund by $82,000. That's enough to put $92 in your pocket every week from the time you're 65 until you reach 100.

• *Take from the IRS; give to your 401(k).* If, like most taxpayers, you get a refund from the IRS every year, your employer is withholding more taxes than necessary from your paycheck. Since you're already accustomed to living without that extra income, why not save it instead? You'll have to do without the refund check you've been getting from the IRS each summer. But do you even remember what you did with last year's refund?

To direct the extra tax money into your 401(k), you have to lower the amount you have withheld from your paycheck to a figure closer to the taxes you actually owe. To do that, get the IRS sheet called Form W-4, Withholding Certificate, from your company's payroll department, and increase the number of withholding allowances you claim. (The back of the form includes a worksheet for figuring out the right number; the more allowances, the less tax withheld.) Then increase your 401(k) contributions by roughly the amount you've lowered your tax payments. Just be sure to increase your 401(k) savings before you've had time to get used to the extra money in your check.

Who Gets Your Money?

The other noninvestment decision you'll have to make when you sign up for your 401(k) is who will inherit your account if you die. While this is a seemingly routine request, it has been made more complicated by a well-meaning law meant to protect widows. This rule requires that the money in your 401(k) go to your surviving spouse—even if you name someone else as heir in your enrollment form or in your will. The only way to name someone besides your spouse is to ask your spouse to consent to the change in writing before a notary public. A prenuptial agreement doesn't count, either, since the law specifically says the change must be made by the spouse. Your betrothed, however compliant he or she may be in the prenuptial agreement, isn't your spouse until you're married.

You have to be extra sure that your 401(k) paperwork is in order if your family is more complicated than the traditional Ozzie and Harriet pairing. If you have remarried, make sure that your benefits administrator has the name of your current spouse on file. And if you want someone besides your spouse to get your money, make sure that the benefits folk get a properly documented spousal waiver form. Your 401(k) is supposed to provide a comfortable retirement for you—or for your heirs if you can't be around to enjoy it. You should make sure that you don't instead provide your heirs with a legal migraine.

KEY POINTS

- To make the most of your 401(k), enroll as early as you can for as much as you can afford.
- Just about the only 401(k) plan you should avoid is one that offers the company stock as the only investment choice.
- Before you start fully funding your 401(k), you should have an emergency reserve fund equal to three to six months' living expenses.
- You should contribute at least as much as your company will match.
- If you can afford to, you should kick in additional money on a pretax basis unless you really aren't sure that you can keep the money invested until retirement. In that case, make after-tax contributions, if your plan permits.
- Remember that your spouse is your account's sole beneficiary unless your spouse waives his or her right to your money in writing.

CHAPTER 5

The Five Principles of Smart Investing

Investing well is only part of the job of managing your 401(k) successfully. But without a doubt, it's the part that creates the most ulcers. Benefits administrators say that the most urgent question they get from 401(k) participants is: "Where should I put my money?" (Unfortunately it's the one question they will never answer.) And in a 1994 *Worth/ Roper* survey, 28% of the respondents cited making a mistake with a major investment as one of the things in life that causes them the most anxiety. Investing was chosen more often than any other potential anxiety provoker, including major surgery, being audited by the IRS, and seeing your spouse flirt with someone else.

While it's heartening that people have such faith in their doctors and their spouses (I'm not so sure, though, about the IRS), there's no reason investing should be so high on the worry list. Granted, people in the investment biz tend to speak in jargon, which can be intimidating to novices. But investment-speak, like jargon in other fields, is often only a way to lend an air of gravity to ideas that are nothing more than common sense when stated in plain English.

It's also true that a lot of smart people spend a lot of time trying to predict how investment markets will perform in the next quarter or six months, and then go on television or into print to announce their latest forecast (while saying nothing about last quarter's absolutely wrong-headed prediction). All this preening and prognosticating is just the froth atop the serious but simple process of investing. But many people have the impression that it is the real essence of intelligent money management, and if you don't know how to do it, you can't handle a 401(k).

Not true. The key to investing wisely isn't knowing a lot of complicated facts. Instead it's mainly a matter of applying a few basic truths consistently for a long time. To stretch a metaphor a bit, investing is like exercising. You could get a Ph.D. in physical education and know a lot more than the average jogger about cardiovascular capacity. But if you want to get into shape there's no substitute for showing up at the gym day after day and working out—and you don't need any special knowledge to do that. Similarly, what really counts in managing your 401(k) is how you apply the simple principles discussed in this chapter. Doing that isn't necessarily easy: it takes patience, perseverance, and a certain amount of self-control. But it doesn't require a Wall Street address, a set of power suspenders, or a Harvard MBA.

But before we get into a discussion of wise investing principles, let's look at some basics about the process itself.

What Investing Is

People who are dubious about investing sometimes prefer to direct their money to so-called socially responsible investments—typically, stocks in firms that don't pollute or support abortion or that have lots of women or minorities on their boards of directors. But the fact is, investing is a socially responsible activity in itself. It requires that you sacrifice some gratification today in the interests of not becoming a burden on your fellow citizens in the future. That surely meets some standard of civic responsibility.

From an economist's point of view, investing is socially constructive because it recycles your savings back into the economy in a way that makes the economy more productive. Private enterprises need money to build new factories and laboratories, create new jobs, buy more efficient machines, and so on. That money comes from ordinary people's savings and investments. If people don't save enough, the economy will starve for capital and the country's standard of living will stagnate. That's one reason the Treasury is willing to forgo taxing the portion of your salary that you contribute to your 401(k). Uncle Sam knows that the economy needs the money.

But of course, while investing does society good, it's not a charitable activity. As an investor, you get a return on the money you invest. In essence, you share in the wealth you've helped to create.

How You Keep Score in This Game

Any discussion of investment performance inevitably leads to lots of numbers with percentage signs after them. But if you're new to the investing game, it may not be entirely clear exactly what those numbers mean. Here's an explanation.

The goal in investing your 401(k) is to get the biggest return on your money—basically, to get the most money back for the money you contribute. Return is usually measured as a percentage of the money you put in. So if you invest $100 and five years later you have $200, you received a return of $100, or 100% of your original stake.

The only problem is that people tend to think of returns in annual terms. That's the way the bank quotes you the interest rate on a savings account, for example: it's 5% per year. So returns over periods of several years are usually **annualized**. You look at the starting investment and the final pot of money and figure out what rate of return you'd have had to earn each year to get from point A to point B. For example, you'd need to earn 14.9% a year to turn $100 into $200 in five years. Your *annualized* return would be 14.9%.

Obviously you don't arrive at the annualized return simply by dividing the five-year return of 100% by five years. That's because annualized returns are **compounded**. That means that each year your return is calculated from the amount of money you have at the beginning of the year, not from the original starting amount. So if you earned an even 14.9% a year, your first-year return would have been $14.90 (14.9% of $100); your second year's return would have been $17.12 (14.9% of $114.90); and so on.

To get an annualized return of 14.9%, however, you don't necessarily have to earn exactly 14.9% for five years straight. You would still have an annualized return of 14.9% even if your returns careened from −20% one year to +50% the next, as long as you ended up with $200 after five years. In fact, careening is what most of the higher-returning funds in your 401(k) will do, especially the stock funds. But what matters is what you end up with, not how you got there.

The Three Classes of Assets

There are two ways a company that needs capital can tap into the country's pool of savings. It can borrow from the public by issuing **debt securities**, also known as **fixed-income securities**. These are simply IOUs, in which a borrower agrees to pay a specified interest rate for a set period, at the end of which you get back your **principal**, the money you originally invested. Debt securities are broken into two separate classes, depending on how much time remains before the debt must be paid off. Those that mature in a matter of weeks or months are known as **cash equivalents** or simply **cash**. Those that remain outstanding longer are known as **notes** or **bonds**.

The other way for a company to raise capital is to sell part ownership in itself by issuing shares of stock (also known as **equity securities**) to the public. Once an investor buys fixed-income securities or equities from a company, he or she is free to sell them to other investors, and in fact, the vast majority of securities traded on a given day change hands between investors, rather than between investors and issuers.

Most 401(k)s include all three investment classes—cash, bonds, and equities—among their investment options. However, few plans expect you to invest in the securities directly. Most of the time you buy shares—your 401(k) may refer to them as **units**—in funds that invest in them for you. In some respects, being one step removed in this way is different from owning the securities directly, particularly with fixed-income securities. (We'll explain how in Chapter 8.) But for the most part, investing through a fund gives you all the rewards and risks of owning the securities directly.

How Investors Make Money

Debt holders and equity investors collect their rewards in different ways. With debt securities, virtually all of your return consists of the interest rate the borrower has agreed to pay. So as long as you hold the security until it matures— and the issuer doesn't default—you know exactly what you will get. But be careful: a debt security isn't just another form of bank account. The market prices of bonds and notes do go up and down between the issue date and maturity, and if you sell before maturity, you could lose principal— a fact that many novice investors learn the hard way.

That's why what really matters to a fixed-income investor is a security's **total return**—income *plus* any change in price—not just its interest rate. (If the concept of total return still seems a little slippery, take a look at page 69, "Will the Real Return Please Stand Up?") We'll go into the reasons fixed-income securities fluctuate in Chapter 8. For now, keep in mind that because the returns on debt securities can *in theory* be mapped out in advance, they are generally much safer and more predictable than stocks.

When you own stock funds in your 401(k), you get to take part in all the thrills and chills of owning a business (or of owning many businesses, since no 401(k) fund would invest in only one stock unless it was set up specifically to invest in your employer's shares). And like an owner, you can be rewarded in two ways: the cash the business throws off, if any—paid to stock investors in the form of a **dividend**—and any increase, or **appreciation**, in the value of the shares. So, like a fixed-income investor, a stock holder is also concerned with total return.

The difference, however, is that the lion's share of the total return (or loss) in a stock comes from changes in the price of the stock. If the outlook for the company that issued your stock has improved since you bought it, other investors will be willing to buy it from you for more than you paid. If you sell at that point, you make a profit, or **capital gain**. If the stock's prospects have worsened, the price will go down. If you sell at that point, you'll have a loss.

Will the Real Return Please Stand Up?

Every 401(k) bond fund has a yield, as does every money-market fund and even most stock funds. But ignore that. The figure that best tells you how successful your funds have been is the **total return**.

Total return consists of the income your fund earns (meaning interest from bonds and dividends from stocks that the fund owns) plus the changes in your fund's share price or unit price (which reflects changes in the value of the fund's stocks and bonds). So if your bond fund starts the year at $10 a share, yields 7%, and has an ending value of $10.50, your total return is 12% (the 7% yield plus the 5% price appreciation).

Economists add one more twist to this calculation by subtracting from it the rate of inflation. What they end up with is called **real total return**, or just **real return**. In the previous example, if inflation during the year had been 4%, your bond fund's real total return would have been 8% (12% total return minus 4% inflation). In other words, in terms of your actual power to buy the things you need, your bond fund left

---

you 8% better off than when you started the year. Though your quarterly statements almost certainly don't cite your 401(k) account's real return (for one thing, no one is exactly sure what inflation has been until long after the fund returns are tallied), it may be the most meaningful figure in the end.

Principle No. 1: All Investments Carry Risk

The minute you put a dollar into your 401(k), you are taking a chance with it. This is not unique to 401(k)s. It would be just as true if you were to put the money into your bank account or under your mattress. Investors like to think of some investments as free of risk. But like it or not, the clock starts ticking on every dollar as soon as you earn it.

The investment risk is obvious in your 401(k)'s stock funds. In the stock market crash of 1987, for example, stocks lost 36% of their value between late August and early November. Roughly $1 trillion that people thought they had in their brokerage accounts, mutual funds, pension funds, or 401(k) accounts simply vaporized. The chance that you might lose money this way is what the experts call **principal risk**. It's what most investors mean when they talk about risk.

The way to avoid principal risk is fairly straightforward: Just keep all your money in cash investments like your 401(k)'s money-market fund. But these steady-going investments leave you wide open to another pitfall: **inflation risk**. This is basically the possibility that as your dollars sit around in their money-market fund (or wherever), inflation will erode their value faster than their interest rate adds to them.

To see just how vulnerable cash investments can be, take a look at the long-term record in the chart on page 75.

70

According to the Chicago research firm Ibbotson Associates, cash has returned some 3.7% a year since 1926, even as inflation ran at 3.2%. Economists would say that the "real" return for that period—the return minus the inflation rate—was a mere 0.5%. But much of the time it wasn't even *that* good. Over all the 10-year periods between 1931 and 1997 (that is, 1931–1941, 1932–1942, and so on), interest rates on cash investments failed to keep up with the rate of increase in consumer prices about half the time. When you figure that the meager returns on cash will eventually be eroded even further by taxes when you withdraw your 401(k) money, it's clear that the investments most 401(k) participants think of as their plan's safest may actually be the most dangerous in the long run.

The investment that offers the best antidote to inflation risk is, paradoxically, the one that carries the most principal risk: stocks. Despite the occasional market crash, from 1926 through 1997 stocks returned seven percentage points a year more than the inflation rate. And over all those 10-year stretches between 1931 and 1997, stock *never* failed to beat inflation.

The choice you face in investing your 401(k), then, isn't between safe funds and risky funds. It's between taking principal risk and taking inflation risk. Which makes more sense: to take a chance of losing principal in hopes of getting a return that trounces inflation, or to trade the possibility of losing money for the near certainty of seeing your money eroded by inflation? If the answer isn't obvious already, it should be by the time you finish the next principle.

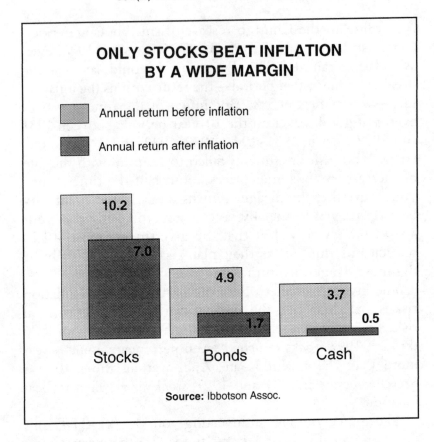

**ONLY STOCKS BEAT INFLATION
BY A WIDE MARGIN**

Annual return before inflation

Annual return after inflation

	Stocks	Bonds	Cash
Before inflation	10.2	4.9	3.7
After inflation	7.0	1.7	0.5

Source: Ibbotson Assoc.

Principle No. 2: In the Long Run, It Pays to Take Principal Risk

From the press coverage of the financial markets, there seems to be little difference between putting your money in stocks and putting it into slot machines in Las Vegas. One day the Dow Jones Industrial Average falls by 82 points and the TV experts begin to make ominous predictions about serious losses to come. Two days later the Dow is up 65 and the same experts are back on television, chirping optimistically about the market's resilience. From one day to the next it seems as if the stock market (and to a lesser extent the bond market as well) is completely random. That's because it is. From one day—or week, or even year—to the next, the markets are no more predictable than a roll of the dice.

Over the long run, however, the markets do obey a fairly strict and predictable rule: The returns you can expect are roughly proportionate to the principal risk you take. In the long run, bonds have always returned more than cash and stocks have always returned more than bonds. Every financial adviser knows these numbers by heart: since 1926, stocks have provided returns equal to 10.2% a year, while bonds have returned 4.9% and cash investments just 3.7%.

Why does it play out this way? Because prices for securities are set in a generally open, competitive marketplace. Think of the financial markets as a kind of supermarket, except that you shop for return and you pay for it in risk. Just as no informed shopper would pay $10 for a loaf of bread at one store when loaves are selling down the street for $1.25, no informed investor would take the risk of buying a stock if he could get almost the same return from a relatively safe bond or cash. Obviously, investors as a whole are not always right about the outlook for stocks, bonds, and cash, but in the long run this sort of financial cantaloupe-squeezing assures that the "price" of a certain asset tends to be fair.

Principle No. 3: Patience Pays

When economists or financial writers (including this one) pronounce some principle of investment, they usually hedge themselves with the words "in the long run." There's a reason. Economists base their theories on the idea that investors act rationally in their own interests. But in the day-to-day or even year-to-year emotion of the markets, all rational bets are off.

In theory, principle number two decrees that the stock market should outperform bonds because stocks carry a greater risk of principal loss. That's true in the long run, but in any given year the chance that stocks will beat bonds or cash is about six out of 10, or little better than a coin toss. As you lengthen your holding period, however, the odds that your returns will line up as expected get dramatically better. For example, over five-year holding periods, stocks outperform bonds 70% of the time and cash about 75%. Over 20-year periods, stocks have the edge over bonds in 94% of the cases and over cash in 99%. And young investors, take note: There has *never* been a 30-year period in this country since 1871 in which stocks have not outperformed both bonds and cash.

As a practical matter, this means that when you take on principal risk in your 401(k), you should expect to go through patches when it doesn't seem to pay off. Both stocks and bonds will suffer some nerve-jangling declines. At these moments you will probably be tempted to kick yourself for not having all your money in your plan's safest investments. If so, remember that these stretches have occurred regularly in the financial markets without altering the fact that higher-risk investments usually give higher returns in the long run—and the longer you hold on, the more likely you are to find that "usually" turns to "almost always."

HOLDING STOCKS FOR THE LONG RUN HAS USUALLY PAID OFF

Holding Period	% of Years Since 1871 in Which Stocks Outperformed Bonds	% of Years Since 1871 in Which Stocks Outperformed Cash
1 year	59%	64%
2 years	64	69
5 years	71	75
10 years	82	84
20 years	94	99
30 years	100	100

Source: *Stocks for the Long Run* by Jeremy J. Siegel, Irwin Professional Publishing, Burr Ridge, Illinois.

Principle No. 4: Spreading Your Money Around Will Lower Your Risk

The principle that your long-term return is commensurate with the risks you take is the bedrock rule of investing. But there is a way to bend the rule. The secret: to spread your money around among the different funds in your 401(k). That can often deliver a higher return while actually lowering your overall risk. For example, adding stocks to a portfolio made up entirely of bonds is able not only to give the portfolio a higher return, but also to lower the portfolio's risk. That's true even though stocks tend to be riskier than bonds. This is known as the **diversification effect**. We'll look more closely at the benefits and techniques of diversification in Chapter 10.

Risky Business

Everyone intuitively understands risk. It's the chance that your investments won't turn out the way you want them to, for whatever reason. But that intuitive definition doesn't help you much when you're trying to compare multimillion-dollar investment funds, each with scores of stocks in its investment portfolio. How can you tell which has more risk?

Financial theorists have come up with two ways of quantifying investing's four-letter word. In both cases, what is measured is the tendency of the fund's returns to swing widely from one period to the next, its **volatility**. The simpler of the two is known as **beta**, which compares the severity of fluctuations in the fund's returns with those of some market benchmark. For most domestic stock funds, the benchmark is the S&P 500. So if a stock fund and the S&P 500 tend to be equally fitful in their returns, the fund is said to have a beta of 1.0. If the fund typically rises and falls 1.5 percentage points for every one point move in the index, it has a beta of 1.5.

The other common risk measure is **standard deviation**, a term borrowed from statistics. It measures how varied the fund's returns are from one period to the next. A standard deviation of 10 means that roughly two-thirds of a fund's total returns over a specified period fall in a range 10 percentage points above or 10 points below the fund's average return for the whole period. So if a fund had a 10% annualized return over 10 years with a standard deviation of 10, the fund's yearly returns normally ranged from 0% (10% average return, minus the standard deviation) to 20%.

Neither measure is ideal. Both, for example, penalize the fund for sharp moves, even if the move is upward. Also, both cover only past performance, which means that they cannot reveal latent but as yet unrealized pitfalls. Still, beta and standard deviation are the best measures thus far for quantifying the slippery concept of risk.

Principle No. 5: No One Knows More Than You Do about the Future

Every time the stock or bond market makes a major move, the air waves are filled with well-dressed experts confidently predicting the level of the market in six months or a year.

Learned as these experts may seem, you should regard what you hear mainly as entertainment. The fact is, if you understand that in the long run stocks tend to beat bonds, and bonds tend to beat cash, you know as much as the experts do about the markets' direction.

It's true that sometimes investors can have specialized knowledge about a particular company that can give them an edge over other investors. If you work in shipping for a computer manufacturer, for example, and the boss has just ordered an extra shift to keep up with demand, you may have an insight into your company's short-term prospects. But not even those articulate folks on *Wall Street Week* have any particular foreknowledge of what the overall stock and bond markets are going to do from one week or one year to the next. If they did, they would be too busy trading stocks to go on TV and talk about it.

In fact, savvy investors tend to get nervous when a majority of experts agree about the market's direction—because they are so often wrong. According to Investor's Intelligence, a research service that tracks optimism or pessimism among investment newsletters, the expert consensus is the most misguided just when it matters most—right before a major turn in the market. For example, only 20% of newsletter editors foresaw the crash of 1987, when the market fell 36%. Equally discouraging, only 31% of these supposed savants were calling for a rally in late 1990, just before stocks went on a three-year 68% tear.

To be fair to the professionals, contrary behavior is in the nature of financial markets. When everyone agrees that stocks, say, are a great investment, it means that everyone has bought all the stocks they plan to buy. At that point there's no demand left from new investors to continue driving up the price of equities. Sooner or later something will happen to shake investors' optimism, and the market will fall. While this simplifies the explanation somewhat, the phenomenon is common wisdom on Wall Street: in the

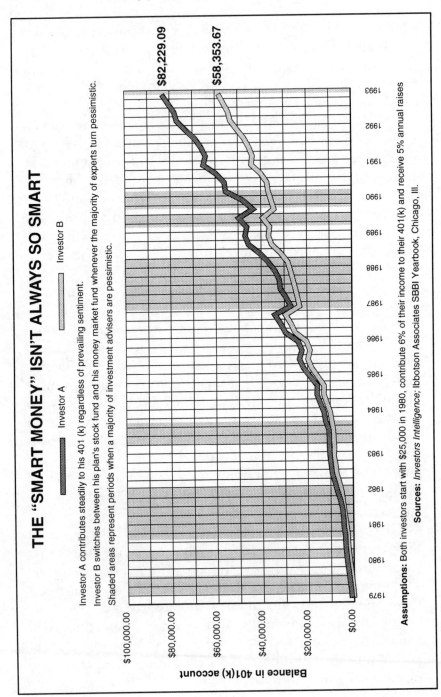

THE "SMART MONEY" ISN'T ALWAYS SO SMART

Investor A   Investor B

Investor A contributes steadily to his 401 (k) regardless of prevailing sentiment.
Investor B switches between his plan's stock fund and his money market fund whenever the majority of experts turn pessimistic.
Shaded areas represent periods when a majority of investment advisers are pessimistic.

$82,229.09

$58,353.67

Assumptions: Both investors start with $25,000 in 1980, contribute 6% of their income to their 401(k) and receive 5% annual raises

Sources: *Investors Intelligence;* Ibbotson Associates SBBI Yearbook, Chicago, Ill.

Balance in 401(k) account

$100,000.00
$80,000.00
$60,000.00
$40,000.00
$20,000.00
$0.00

1979 1980 1981 1982 1983 1984 1985 1986 1987 1988 1989 1990 1991 1992 1993

short run, the market frequently does the opposite of what the majority expects it to do.

For 401(k) investors, the first step to achieving investing wisdom is knowing what can't be known—by you or anyone else. Don't let yourself be swayed by talk show jabber or by occasional short-term hiccups in the market. Instead you should be willing to take some risks, especially by investing in your plan's stock funds, and then stick with that decision for the long haul. That is the foundation of smart investing, and in the long run, it's the surest way to build a giant 401(k).

Benchmarks, Indexes, and Other Bogies

A fund's total return tells you how the fund is doing compared with its starting point, and real return tells you how well the fund is standing up to inflation. But how do you judge how well the fund is doing against its peers? A 15% return in a year sounds fine all by itself, but it would be mediocre if everyone else had earned 20%—and by the same token, it would be brilliant if everyone else had lost money.

To keep fund managers honest, investment pros compare fund returns to benchmarks known as market indexes. Indexes are collections of securities chosen by research firms not because they are good investments, but rather because they are representative of the market as a whole or a specific sector of the market.

The most famous of these yardsticks is the Dow Jones Industrial Average, which is universally used as an informal synonym for the stock market. (When someone says the market was up 29 points yesterday, they are talking about the Dow Jones Industrial Average.) Professionals, however, tend to regard the Standard & Poor's 500 stock index—which consists of 500 large and medium-size domestic companies from all industries—as more representative of the stock market, or at least the market for large-company stocks. There are similar indexes for international stocks, small-company stocks, bonds, and so on. To calculate the "return" of an index, researchers simply average together the returns of all the securities that make up the index. (This is oversimplified, but it's the basic idea.)

The beauty of a benchmark is that it allows you to gauge what professional money managers contribute to your fund's return. If the S&P 500 returned 5% for the quarter but your 401(k)'s equity fund lost 5% (or made 20%), it could mean that your manager is concentrating on particular stocks whose returns diverged from the average. That could signal a riskier approach than you may have realized you were taking.

Many 401(k) funds include funds that do nothing but attempt to match the return of the index—sometimes simply by buying every security represented in the index. If your plan offers them, these so-called index funds can be a great foundation for your 401(k) strategy, since they essentially guarantee you a return that matches "the market." As you will discover in Chapter 6, not every professionally managed fund can make the same claim.

KEY POINTS

- Successful 401(k) investing doesn't require any particular investing expertise. But it does call for familiarity with a few basic investing principles.
- The main choice in your 401(k) isn't between safe and risky investments; it's between taking on short-term principal risk and long-term inflation risk.
- To beat inflation in the long run, you must take principal risk.
- Don't let short-term market setbacks or "expert" advice distract you from your long-term strategy.
- Spread your money around to minimize principal risk.

CHAPTER 6

Going for Growth with Stock Funds

If taking any one step can turn you from a saver into a true investor, it's putting your money into the stock market. Owning shares in corporations transforms you from a mere spectator into an active participant in the drama of free enterprise. The profitability of American business ceases to be something you can dismiss as merely the preoccupation of people in suits: suddenly it makes a difference to your personal financial security as well. And that can change the way you look at a lot of things. Once your own capital is at stake, after all, you're a capitalist. You may actually start thinking like one. You may, heaven help you, even catch yourself occasionally reading the business pages.

Of course, none of this is any reason to put your money into your 401(k)'s stock funds. The real reason is quite simple: Stocks give you the best shot at the highest returns you're likely to earn in your 401(k). Over periods of a decade or more, stocks have consistently outperformed all the other investments you're likely to encounter in your plan—in fact, all other kinds of investments, period, including gold, real estate, rare coins, baseball cards, you name it. And market historians tell us that stocks have done so for nearly two centuries.

Even so, nearly a third of 401(k) investors don't have a penny in their stock funds. That's a bad mistake, and one you should not repeat. As long as you are more than five years from needing the money in your plan, stock funds ought to be at the core of your 401(k) investment strategy.

The Case for Stocks

The cardinal rule of investing—that you must take prudent risk if you hope to get decent returns—is utterly borne out by the performance of U.S. equities. The numbers speak for themselves.

• One dollar invested in large-company stocks at the end of 1925 was worth more than $1,113 at the end of 1995. The same dollar invested in riskier small companies grew to more than $3,822. The closest competitor outside of the stock market, long-term corporate bonds, turned $1 into just $48.
• Over long periods the stock market's trend has been relentlessly upward. Although the market goes through phases in which stock prices fall ("bear markets" in Wall Street jargon), the rising phases ("bull markets") tend to last longer and go farther. According to the stock market almanac *101 Years on Wall Street*, the average postwar bull lasted 38 months and nearly doubled stock investors' money, on average, each time. The average bear market lasted only 14 months and cost investors just 27%.
• Need further evidence? How's this for a clincher: Since

1926, the equity market's *worst* 30-year return was nearly *three times* as good as the bond market's *best* return.

Why do so many 401(k) holders nevertheless avoid stocks? One reason may be that they are focusing too much on the risks. The stock market makes it into some people's consciousness only when it shows up on the evening news—usually after a major sell-off. That has led many noninvestors to form a completely unwarranted opinion of the market's risks. According to a survey by the money-management firm Oppenheimer & Co., nearly half of Americans believe that most stock investors are "wiped out" at least once in their career.

Nonsense. In the past 123 calendar years, stocks posted negative returns just 36 times. In other words, in three years out of four, stock investors got richer. In only six of the past 123 years were there downturns greater than 20%, and even then the markets usually recovered swiftly and permanently. For example, had you put your money into stocks the day before the crash in 1987—when stocks plunged 23% in a single day—you would have been back to even within 13 months. As the chart on page 85 suggests, often the worst thing you can do as an investor is to pull out of stocks just when it is most tempting to do so—after they take a pronounced tumble.

Besides, looking at stocks in one-year blocks tends to exaggerate their true risks. Over longer periods stock returns are actually more predictable than other investments. Over 30-year stretches going back to 1926, for example, stocks' average annual rates of return have varied from a high of 13.5% to a low of 8.6% a year. That's almost as narrow a range of returns as bonds and cash achieved over the same series of 30-year periods.

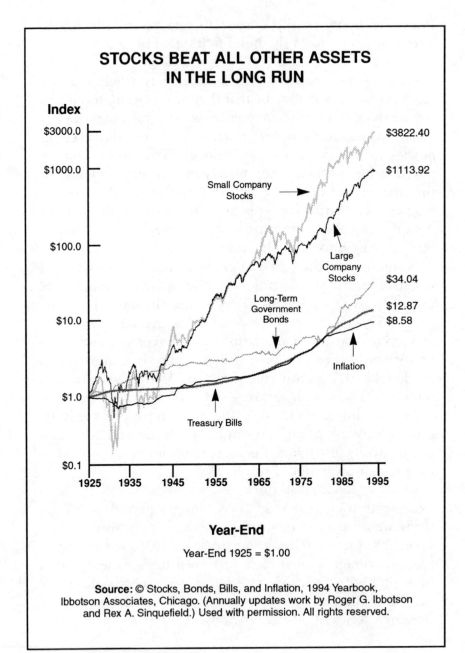

STOCKS BEAT ALL OTHER ASSETS IN THE LONG RUN

Year-End

Year-End 1925 = $1.00

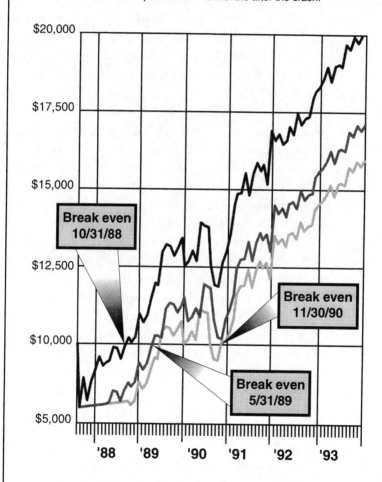

IT PAYS TO STICK WITH STOCKS, EVEN DURING ROUGH PATCHES

— Investor A stays fully invested through the 1987 crash.
— Investor B pulls out of stocks for six months after the crash.
⋯ Investor C pulls out for 12 months after the crash.

Break even
10/31/88

Break even
11/30/90

Break even
5/31/89

$20,000
$17,500
$15,000
$12,500
$10,000
$5,000

'88 '89 '90 '91 '92 '93

Assumptions: All three investors have $10,000 in their account on October 19, 1987, the day of the market crash.

Source: *The Independent T. Rowe Price Adviser*

But Will the Future Be a Replay of the Past?

Is there any guarantee that stocks will continue to rise in the future? No, of course not. But there is no reason to think that the future will diverge dramatically from the patterns of the past. Stock market historian Jeremy J. Siegel and author of the excellent book *Stocks for the Long Run* notes that stock market returns have been remarkably consistent over long periods (40 years plus) all the way back to 1802, with the average annual returns ranging from 6.6% to 7.0% above the inflation rate over each measuring period. Siegel speculates that investors demand roughly that rate of return, consciously or not, to justify taking the short-term risks of stock investing. If 6% or so after inflation seems temporarily unattainable, investors will take their money elsewhere. Eventually that will cause stock prices to drop to a point at which that rate once again seems within reach—and investors will pile back into the market.

Other experts point out that stocks can't fail to prosper as long as U.S. corporations do. Equities, after all, aren't just curios that can go out of fashion, like a Willie Mays baseball card; they are legal interests in real, money-making enterprises. So an investment in a stock fund is essentially a bet that U.S. corporations as a whole will continue to find a way to boost profits. Is that a reasonable wager? It certainly seems so: the industriousness and creativity that brought the world the Pentium microchip, *Jurassic Park*, and Federal Express show no sign of drying up anytime soon. You should avoid stocks only if you're convinced for some reason that Americans have lost the knack for making money. To most people, *that* sounds farfetched.

True, there is no certainty that stocks will continue to be the best investment choice for 401(k)s. But in the investment world, you cannot afford to wait for absolute certainty before acting. The best you can do in plotting a strategy for your financial future is to play the odds. And the odds are overwhelming that stocks, the runaway best investment over most periods in the past, will also be your best choice over the one period in the future that really matters: the one that stretches from now until you retire.

How Stocks Work

Buying shares in a corporation makes you part owner of that corporation, entitled to your proportionate share of its assets and any dividends the company pays out. Normally, you even have a minor say in how the company is run, since your shares give you the right to elect the board of directors and vote on other business decisions. (Unless you are a big shareholder, of course, no one will pay too much attention.) If the company were to run into financial difficulty, however, the shareholders would occupy the last spot in the creditors' line. Shareholders get only what is left after debt holders are paid off—which is usually nothing.

On the other hand, stock investors stand to profit from their position in two ways. The more secure part of a stock's total return comes from **dividends**, a portion of profits that the company splits with shareholders. Companies typically pay out half or less of their profits in dividends. Slow-growth outfits like utilities may pay out 80% or more, while fast-growing small businesses may pay no dividend at all, preferring to reinvest all their profits in the business.

As of late 1997, the **dividend yield** on the average large-company stock stood about 1.7%. (Dividend yield is the annual dividend divided by the stock's current price.) That's a very low yield by historical standards. Since World War II, large companies have paid a dividend averaging around 4.5% of the share price, which means that dividends accounted for nearly half of the market's overall 11.4% annual return over the period. The dividend yield has gone as high as 7%, however, when stock prices were badly depressed, as they were in late 1974.

A dividend is not as secure a return as interest on a bond, since the company is perfectly entitled to cut or even eliminate its dividend if cash gets tight. (By contrast, a company can't unilaterally cut the interest payments on a bond without going into default.) But most companies are very reluctant to take that step since it is a sure sign of financial distress.

As mentioned in the previous chapters, the bulk of a stockholder's return has historically come from appreciation in the price of his shares. Appreciation is far less predictable than dividend payments because so much rests on investors' fickle frame of mind. Unlike a bond, a stock doesn't carry a promise to repay the investors' principal at any future date. So a stock's price generally represents nothing more than investors' collective judgment about the stock's profit potential over the next several years. Companies that are widely believed to be able to increase earnings at 15% or more command a high price in relation to last year's earnings or next year's anticipated earnings. Stocks with less rosy outlooks trade at a lower relative price.

Investors measure this relative value by dividing the market price by the company's expected annual earnings. Known as the **price–earnings multiple**, or **P/E**, this is the single most important gauge of a stock's worth. When a professional refers to a stock as expensive or cheap, she is referring not to whether it trades for $10 a share or $100, but rather to its P/E. The figure essentially tells you what value the market is willing to put on a dollar of profits from a company right now. Not surprisingly, the rights to those profits are worth more if you expect them to grow to, say, $1.25 a share next year (a 25% earnings growth rate) than if you can't see them getting beyond $1.05 (a 5% growth rate).

Why the Stock Market Fluctuates

If the stock market operated under laboratory conditions, stock prices would perfectly reflect changes in corporate earnings. In other words, if corporate profits overall rose 10%, the market would return 10%. But of course, it's not remotely that simple. Investors are continuously reevaluating their outlook in light of a constant barrage of new information. The market's dominant emotion can swing from deepest gloom to brightest euphoria—and vice versa, of course—at the release of some government economic statistic, at some delphic pronouncement by the chairman of the Federal Reserve Board, at an unexpected development at a major corporation, or for no apparent reason at all.

Most of the news that makes the market jump isn't very significant in itself. What gets stock traders' juices flowing is the notion that certain news flashes shed light on the future course of the two economic factors that most affect the stock market as a whole: interest rates and the economy's intermittent swings between expansion and recession. Both have a powerful effect on the stock market, and not even the most carefully selected 401(k) fund portfolio is immune to them.

It probably doesn't strike you as startling news that the economy's inevitable cycle between recession and expansion—often called the **business cycle**—has an enormous impact on the stock market. Obviously a healthy, expanding economy is good for profits, and a recession isn't. Accordingly, the stock market has a penchant for going into a funk a few months before recessions occur. It typically resumes its upward trend a few months before the recession ends, as the economic outlook starts to brighten.

The stock market also keeps an eye on interest rates, since that helps determine whether stocks seem like a good buy in relation to other investments. For example, when the interest rate on Treasury notes is 5%, the prospect that profits at major corporations might grow, say, 15% looks pretty good. The same earnings growth looks less delectable when interest rates are 12%. In that case, an investor could get almost as much bang if he put his money into Treasuries, and he'd take far less principal risk.

One caution: Knowing *why* the stock market rises and falls is not the same as knowing *when* it will do so. It's awfully tempting to try to "time" your 401(k) fund investing by trying to forecast interest rates and turns in the business cycle. That way you could buy into and cash out of your 401(k)'s stock funds in advance of big moves in the market. But save yourself the trouble. No one has a crystal ball. Despite the billions of dollars that Wall Street spends each year on forecasting the economy, the majority of experts miss as many major turning points as they catch.

The real point is that the forces that move the market are cyclical. Recessions happen, but they are ultimately followed by recoveries. Interest rates go up, but they always eventually come down. Likewise, though the stock market tumbles periodically, it always bounces back. Keeping that in mind will help you hang on to your 401(k)'s stock funds when the going gets tough. It's not always easy to do, but that's what it takes to make money in stocks in the long run.

How Stock Funds Work

The typical stock fund in your 401(k) is simply a collection of stocks gathered together under the direction of a professional money manager. As an investor, you own your share of this package, and all the rewards and risks pass through to you just as if you directly owned a small piece of each of the stocks in the portfolio. You receive a proportionate share of the total dividends the portfolio throws off as well as any price appreciation (or loss) that the portfolio as a whole achieves. The fund's return is simply the collective return of all the stocks in the portfolio.

There are some important advantages to owning your stocks this way, rather than picking them one at a time. One of them is that you get much greater diversification than you could afford on your own, thus eliminating the risk that an unforeseen disaster in just one stock will trip up your fund's overall performance. (Diversification is explained in more detail in Chapter 10.) Whether you are contributing your first $100 or already have $50,000 invested, you become part owner of the same dozens or hundreds of stocks as every other investor in the fund. For example, Fidelity Asset Manager, a popular publicly sold mutual fund found in many 401(k) plans, owns 1,000 stocks. Since you generally buy stocks in lots of 100 shares, you'd need about $2.5 million to buy that many different issues on your own.

Another major advantage is that your fund is run by a professional investment manager, who relieves you of much of the day-to-day work of investing. The manager takes responsibility for handling the flow of cash from 401(k) participants into and out of the fund, choosing and buying stocks, monitoring their performance, and, most difficult, selling at the most propitious moment. That means you can expect to receive competitive returns from your stock investments, even if you don't know anything about the stock market.

You do have to pay for that service, of course. The manager subtracts a fee that works out to between 0.5% and 2.0% of the fund's assets each year, depending on the type of fund it is. This fee reduces your return, percentage point for percentage point. For example, if the fee is 1% and the securities that the fund owns collectively went up 10% for the year, the fund will show a return of 9%. If the stocks in the portfolio went down 10%, the fund's loss would be 11%. All else equal, 401(k) investors should prefer funds with lower expenses.

Types of Stock Funds

Not all stock funds invest alike, which is why most 401(k)s give you a choice of several. Some zero in on the riskiest sectors of the market in hopes of earning top-flight returns. Others ply a conservative course, aiming to give a shot at equity returns to investors who don't have the stomach for taking high principal risk. The riskier types tend to favor the stocks of smaller companies and rely almost exclusively on capital appreciation for their return. More conservative funds lean toward the stocks of larger companies and often aim to have a substantial income component to their return. Most of the funds you're likely to encounter in your plan fall into one of the categories sketched below. For a more detailed side-by-side comparison of the different types, see the table on page 93.

TYPICAL 401(k) STOCK FUND CHOICES

Fund Type and Typical Investment	Risk Level (Standard Deviation)	% Stocks in Portfolio	% Bonds in Portfolio	Dividend Yield	Annualized Total Return as of Mid-1995		
					One Year	Three Years	Five Years
Aggressive growth: High-risk stocks of up-and-coming new firms	Very high (17.8)	85%	0.5%	0.2%	12.8%	12.1%	11.7%
Growth: Midsize or large-company stocks with solid prospects for appreciation	High (13.1)	89.3	1.0	0.7	13.5	10.3	10.7
Growth and income: Stocks of established, dividend-paying companies	High (11.1)	87.3	2.5	1.7	14.7	10.1	10.1
Equity index: Strives to replicate the return on a stock market benchmark, often the S&P 500	High (14.2)	95.7	0.0	1.8	14.7	10.3	9.1
Equity income: High-dividend stocks with an emphasis on yield	High (9.8)	79.0	4.5	3.0	13.6	10.0	10.1
International: Fully or largely invested in stocks that trade on foreign exchanges	Very high (14.9)	86.4	1.1	0.4	−2.5	8.5	6.0
Balanced: A mix of large-company stocks and bonds, typically in a 60/40 split	Medium (8.35)	52.9	33.5	2.8	11.5	8.6	9.9
Asset-allocation: A blend of securities of different types, including at least stocks, bonds, and cash	Medium (8.36)	52.1	31.8	2.25	10.5	8.6	9.2

Source: Morningstar Inc., Chicago.

AGGRESSIVE GROWTH FUNDS

Aggressive growth funds have provided the most generous returns over the past 10 years, with an average annual gain of 12.7%. As you would expect, they also subject investors to more principal risk than other types of funds. There also tends to be a wide range of returns among aggressive growth funds: the best are very, very good and the worst are very, very bad. That's one reason only about 25% of 401(k)s offer an aggressive growth choice. It's a good reason for you to approach them with caution, too. If you are bothered by sharp ups and downs in your 401(k) funds, you should put no more than 25% of your account in aggressive funds.

GROWTH FUNDS

Though a notch down in risk from the aggressive category, growth funds still tend to be slightly chancier than standard benchmarks such as the Standard & Poor's 500 or the Dow Jones Industrial Average. Growth funds appear in more than 40% of 401(k)s, and they tend to invest mainly in established fast-growing companies in the consumer, technology, and health care fields. In the plans where they do appear, they are the most popular choice among diversified equity funds, accounting for 15% of the average participant's total balance.

GROWTH AND INCOME

The classic middle-of-the-road equity fund, growth and income funds tend to favor the stocks of large companies that pay dividends. As a whole they are about 10% less volatile than the S&P 500, which makes them a smart choice if you're just getting started in stock funds and a good "core" holding no matter how seasoned an investor you are. (A "core" fund is one you use as a foundation on which to build your 401(k) investing strategy. "The 'Core' Strategy" below explains this idea in detail.) About 45% of all plans include a growth and income option.

The "Core" Strategy

Professionals who invest zillions of dollars for pensions, charitable foundations, and so forth often build their portfolio around what they call **core investments**. It's a way to make their returns more predictable, and it's a technique you may want to emulate in your 401(k).

In a core strategy, you put a portion of the money you intend to allot to equities—half, say—into stock funds that you expect will come close to matching the return and risk of the market as a whole. That way, at least one portion of your 401(k) account is a known quantity compared with the overall market. (Of course, you can't know how the market itself will do from one month or one year to the next; but in the long run you can reasonably count on it to give you a return that beats inflation by a handy margin.) You can then try to add extra return by dividing some or all of the rest of your money among less predictable types of funds, such as aggressive growth funds and internationals. If these high-revving investments fall short of your expectations—that's one of their risks—at least you've locked in a market return on your 401(k)'s core.

Index funds are the perfect choice as core investments, since they are designed to deviate as little as possible from the market's return. If your plan doesn't offer index funds, growth and income entries are a good alternative because they invest in mainstream, established companies in which the likelihood of major shocks—positive or negative—is relatively small.

EQUITY INDEX

These funds differ from other types not so much in the sectors of the stock market where they invest as in their entire investment philosophy. They practice what experts call **passive investing**. Rather than trying to outsmart other investors and select the most promising stocks, an index manager tries simply to imitate the performance of a benchmark like the Standard & Poor's 500. In essence, the manager takes himself and his own views out of the picture and just buys everything in the index—the best stocks, the worst stocks, and everything in between.

While this approach may seem like a copout at first, the record shows that index funds actually consistently deliver above-average returns compared to funds with similar levels of risk. ("The Case for Index Funds" below explains why.) In fact, if your plan's index fund is designed to track the S&P 500—as most are—it makes sense to use it as a foundation of your 401(k)'s stock strategy, much as you would use a growth and income fund. Odds are the index fund will give you the better return.

The Case for Index Funds

Most money managers tend to be competitive people who use their considerable brainpower to pick stocks that they hope will do better than the market as a whole. But managers of index funds are less ambitious. They don't want to beat the market; they just want to match it. Their only goal is to replicate the performance of a market benchmark, like the S&P 500 or the Wilshire 5000. The "average is good enough for me" approach means that no index fund will ever be a top performer.

So why would you ever put any 401(k) money in one? One reason is that it is as difficult to identify consistently top performing funds in advance as it is to predict top performing stocks—and trying to do so sometimes backfires. Choosing an index fund at least eliminates the chance that you will ever be stuck with a doghouse performer. The other reason, surprising as it may seem, is that most conventionally managed funds fail to match the performance of market indexes. For example, of the 426 equity mutual funds that have been in existence for 10 years, just 92 of them managed to beat the S&P 500.

How can portfolios of promising stocks, carefully researched and selected by high-priced Wall Street talent, fail to perform as well as an unmanaged mob of stocks? It may seem puzzling at first, but if you think about it, it's clear why. An index, after all, is designed to represent the market as a whole, or at least a large chunk of it. And the return on the market as a whole is nothing more or less than the collective return of all investors who own stock. In other words, money managers as a group can't beat the market because they *are* the market. Over any period you measure, the return of the average fund should theoretically equal the return of the market.

In real life, however, the average fund isn't even *that* good. That's because real investors have a handicap that an unmanaged index doesn't have: expenses. Real investors have to pay brokerage commissions and, in the case of funds, management fees and operating expenses out of their investment. So an actively managed fund with 1.3% in expenses actually has to outperform the index by 1.3% a year just to keep up with it. The upshot: The average fund's real-life return is almost always *less* than that of the index.

Index funds also have expenses, of course, and they too never quite match the index they are meant to track. But because they don't have to pay money-management fees, they carry expenses as low as 0.2% of assets. That gives a typical index fund an advantage of at least a full percentage point a year over its actively managed competition. That has been enough. Over the past five years, the best-known S&P 500 fund, Vanguard Index 500 Portfolio, has had a higher return than more than 72% of all equity funds.

So if your plan has an index fund, don't scoff at it. Invest in it.

INTERNATIONAL EQUITY

These are essentially growth funds that invest in the stocks of foreign corporations. They have become much more common in 401(k)s—about 60% of plans offered them in 1996—and if your plan has one, it makes sense to put up to 20% or 25% of your account in it. Reason: Foreign markets often rise when U.S. markets are falling, and vice versa. So adding an international fund can smooth out the ups and downs in your account as a whole.

Internationals do have one added element of risk, however. In addition to the normal bumps and bounces of equity markets, international funds expose their investors to **currency risk**. That's the possibility that the foreign currencies in which your fund's stocks are denominated will weaken against the dollar. Say, for example, your fund buys stock in the Japanese carmaker Toyota for 1,600 yen a share at the beginning of the year when the yen is worth 1.2¢ (85 yen to the dollar). Measured in dollars, the stock is worth

$19.20. Let's say the stock finishes the year at 1,650 yen, a rise of 50 yen. But suppose the yen dropped to 1¢ (100 to a dollar) over the same period. At that exchange rate, the stock would be worth just $16.50. So even though the stock showed a slight gain for the year when measured in yen, the currency translation handed you a 14% loss.

Of course, currency risk can cut both ways. In both 1985 and 1986, when foreign currencies were strengthening sharply against the dollar, the average international fund earned in excess of 45%. Much of that gain came from foreign exchange.

BALANCED FUNDS

These hybrids own both stocks and bonds, usually in a roughly 60% stocks, 40% bonds combination. The addition of bonds, a more stable asset than stocks, makes balanced funds less risky than funds that invest entirely in equities— one reason that nearly half of all employers include balanced funds in their 401(k)s, making them the most common kind of equity fund. The deployment of bonds can backfire, however, when fixed-income assets have a dismal year, as they did in 1994, the bond market's worst year since the early 1980s. (Even so, the average balanced fund fell only 2.8% that year.) If your 401(k) doesn't include any separate bond funds, you should probably put some money into a balanced fund. Otherwise you can create your own balanced portfolio by dividing your 401(k) money between a growth and income fund and a bond fund.

ASSET-ALLOCATION FUNDS

Taking the idea of balanced funds a step farther, asset-allocation funds aim to spread your risk over the three main asset categories—stocks, bonds, and cash—and sometimes other investments like foreign bonds and real estate as well. Most managers keep a fairly constant percentage of the fund's money dedicated to each investment category, perhaps making minor adjustments if one seems to have brighter short-term prospects than the others. Because of their cash holdings, asset-allocation funds are even less risky than balanced funds.

LIFE CYCLE FUNDS

These are a fairly new refinement of the asset-allocation funds' one-stop-shopping approach. Like asset-allocation funds, they split your money among the three main investment categories. The difference is that life cycle funds often come with three or more separate portfolios, each with its money proportioned slightly differently among the asset classes. You invest in the portfolio with the biggest equity allotment when you are young and move to the more conservative groupings as you get older and presumably less willing to expose your 401(k) to principal risk.

A Warning about Investing in Your Company's Stock

One other equity investment crops up frequently in 401(k)s, and it happens to be the one that is the most popular with employees: their own employer's stock. About 40% of 401(k) plans offer company stock as one investment option. In those plans, employees have 26% of their total account in the stock, more than twice as much as in growth funds, the next most popular equity investment.

That is a bad idea.

Keeping too much of your money in your employer's stock contradicts the fundamental investing principle of diversification. Keeping 26% of your money in any single security—whether it's your employer's stock, Microsoft stock, or even U.S. Treasury bonds—is unnecessarily risky because the chance always exists that something can go wrong with any investment, no matter how solid it may seem when you buy it. Loading up on a single stock means that you are taking **specific risk**, in addition to the usual principal risk of the stock market. And specific risk is one kind of risk you don't get paid for taking.

In 1972 employees of Xerox Corp., for example, had every reason to think their company was a great investment. It so dominated its market that the corporate name was considered synonymous with photocopiers. But in the 1970s and 1980s the company's products were savaged by Japanese competition, and over the next 20 years—a full career for many people—the stock had an annual return of just 2%. Over the same period, the S&P 500 returned 11.7% a year. Clearly any Xerox worker who invested too heavily in the company's stock regretted it.

While it's bad practice to invest too heavily in any single security, it's doubly perilous when that security is your employer's stock. That's because you already have so much riding on your company's financial health. After all, your job security, your salary, and your medical benefits already depend on your company's fiscal well-being. So does your pension. And if your company is a big employer in town, the value of your house may also depend on your company's continued prosperity.

Granted, as an employee you may have more insight than other investors into the prospects for your company. That can help you pick up shares for your 401(k) when the price is unreasonably low. But even so, don't put more than 10% of your total stock holdings in your employer. Be humble.

In the investment business, there is too much room for unpleasant surprises.

KEY POINTS

- Stock funds should be the foundation of your 401(k) investment strategy. Although they can be risky in the short run, they have consistently offered the highest long-term returns in the past.
- While there is no guarantee that stocks will do as well in the future as they have in the past, it is hard to argue that they will underperform other securities. For one thing, they take more principal risk, so they should offer higher returns. Plus, they give you an *ownership* interest in free enterprise, which remains the world's most powerful engine of prosperity.
- Rather than reaching for astronomical returns by taking excessive risk, you should build your 401(k) strategy around a core of stock investments that promise to deliver returns at least equal to that of the market. Your best bet there, if available: equity index funds.
- Don't put more than 10% of your money in your employer's stock. It's simply too risky.

CHAPTER 7

Sizing Up Your Plan's Stock Funds

How much effort you ought to spend analyzing a plan's stock funds depends a lot on how many stock funds you have. If your plan's only offering is an equity index fund, there isn't much work to do. (You don't spend a lot of time reading the menu if all the restaurant serves is beans.) But the trend in 401(k) plans is to give investors more choice, not less. So even if you're not now confronted with a dozen funds to choose from, you may be one day. In any event, it can't hurt to take a closer look at the funds you do have. The more you understand why they behave as they do, the less likely you are to make an emotional investment decision that you will regret later.

First, one caution about what you should be looking for. It's easy to get the impression that the idea is to find a brilliant money manager who will make you a tall stack of money in a very short time. Such managers get a lot of adoring coverage in the press, and true, it would be neat to have earned 72% last year in Internet stocks, which is often the sort of thing that propels a fund manager to the top.

But if you use Wall Street's latest genius du jour as the standard for judging the success of your 401(k) funds, you are using the wrong yardstick. Most of the managers who earn that title slip back into mediocrity within a few months, as soon as whatever market trend it was that carried them to greatness runs its course.

Investing your 401(k), on the other hand, is a long-term endeavor. You don't want to scramble after flashy performance that quickly fades. As we'll discuss further in Chapter 10, the main determinant of your 401(k)'s total return won't be whether you choose great equity funds or merely good ones; it will be how much of your plan account you devote to equities at all—and how long you stay invested in them.

As a result, your chief goal in analyzing stock funds is to find out how they invest exactly and to make sure that they do it consistently. That way you always know the risk level you are taking and how the funds you own fit together in your investment strategy. As for performance, don't waste your time trying to pick the top dog. It's not possible, and besides, it's not necessary. You should build your retirement plan assuming that you will get average returns. If it turns out you do better, well, you can treat yourself to an extra retirement cruise.

How Fund Managers Size Up Stocks

Like every other kind of shopper, professional investors are always looking for a good value. But shoppers differ about what "value" means. Is it what you get at Nordstrom's, where you pay top dollar but know you are getting good quality and great service? Or is it what's served at Price/ Costco, where the experience is less than elegant but you know the prices are as low as they get?

Money managers differ as well in what defines the best stocks at the best price. Some managers, by inclination or training, are Wall Street's equivalent of the Nordstrom's shopper. They are known as **growth investors**. (And they can be found at the helm of any type of equity fund, not just growth funds.) The ideal growth stock is issued by a company that has everything going for it: strong sales expansion, rising profitability, a clear advantage over its competitors, and no skeletons in the corporate closet. There is a drawback, though, to investing in such premium companies: they tend to sell for premium P/E ratios, and if the stock doesn't live up to investors' rosy expectations, the market can be unforgiving.

Self-styled **value investors**, on the other hand, are the stock market's discount shoppers. They troll for stocks that have fallen out of favor with growth investors—companies in mature industries, like autos or steel, or those on the downside of their own economic cycle, like retailers when consumer spending is slowing down. (Like growth investors, value buyers manage all types of stock funds, even—just to be confusing—some that your 401(k) may call growth funds.) The value investor relies on the fact that when the market turns sour on a stock, it often overshoots, and unloved stocks can often be snapped up at bargain prices in relation to their dividends or their true earning potential. The risk, of course, is that the value investors' unloved stocks will remain unloved, and the fund's return will languish.

Matching the Right Type with the Right Style

It's bad enough having to keep straight whether a fund is an aggressive growth, growth, or growth and income. Now comes the extra layer of investment style: growth vs. value and large company vs. small company. But if style is so important, why aren't funds classified that way to begin with?

Good question. The answer is that a fund's type and its style each tells you something different about how the fund is likely to perform.

The fund categories described in Chapter 6—growth, growth and income, balanced, and so on—give you an idea of the fund's riskiness. They tell you whether the manager aims to get all or most of the fund's return from capital gains or whether he or she leavens the mix with steady income from bonds or dividends. The average aggressive growth fund, for example, owns virtually no bonds and produces a negligible dividend. The average balanced fund, by contrast, devotes a considerable share of its portfolio to bonds and has a dividend yield of nearly 3%.

Style, on the other hand, refers strictly to the character of the stocks that the manager likes to own. It doesn't address whether the manager also owns bonds. As a result, any type of fund can follow any investing style in selecting stocks for its portfolio. (In practice, conservative types like balanced and growth and income funds tend to go for large-company stocks, while aggressive growth funds prefer small stocks; but there's no rule about it.) Style tells you whether you should expect the fund to be doing better or worse than others of its type—as long as you know whether the fund's style is in or out of fashion. Unfortunately, it won't tell you whether or for how long that style will stay in favor. Knowledge of the future, alas, isn't given to mere mortals, however useful it would be for managing our 401(k)s.

This aspect of a manager's taste in stocks—what experts call **investing style**—explains a lot about a fund's return. That's because the two styles tend to take turns outperforming and underperforming each other in cycles that last two to five years. While both growth and value funds tend to make money when the market is up and lose it when the market is sinking, how much they rise or fall depends on which style is in favor.

Similar cycles occur between large stocks and small stocks. While small stocks have the edge overall in performance—as you would expect, since they are higher risk—they don't beat the big guys every year. After walloping large-company stocks in the late 1970s and early 1980s, for example, small-company stocks went into a seven-year hibernation. They regained the upper hand only in recent years, as the economic climate shifted away from the multinational consumer goods companies that ruled the market in the 1980s and back toward small, fast-growing, technology firms. You can see these patterns clearly in the chart on page 107.

While you might think a versatile manager could rise above mere fashion and cherry-pick great stocks regardless of style or size, it rarely happens that way in practice. Most managers tend to stick with what they know best, and that has a tremendous influence on their returns. Studies show that a typical fund's preferences in style and size account for 75% or more of its return. Less than a quarter of the typical fund's performance can be explained solely by the manager's skill (or luck) at choosing stocks within the style. So much for Wall Street wizardry.

As a 401(k) investor, you want to know where your fund's managers stand on the growth vs. value spectrum. If your plan offers funds from both camps, it makes sense to own one of each. That way you're assured of always having one fund that's in style. Even if your plan's selection is more limited, as is often the case, it will be useful to know your funds' style because of the insights that gives you into the fund's performance. Unfortunately you can't always tell from the fund's name where its allegiance lies. You'll have to look a little deeper. The rest of this chapter will tell you how.

How to Size Up a Stock Fund

Finding out about your fund's investment style and other useful information is much easier if the fund is a publicly traded mutual fund than if it's a private fund managed solely for retirement plans. The main reason is that publicly sold mutual funds are regulated by the Securities and Exchange Commission (SEC), whose mantra is full and open disclosure. Other 401(k) investments are governed by Labor De-

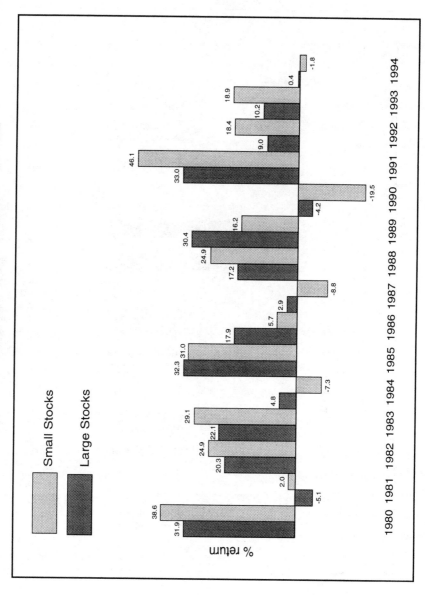

THE IMPORTANCE OF INVESTMENT STYLE

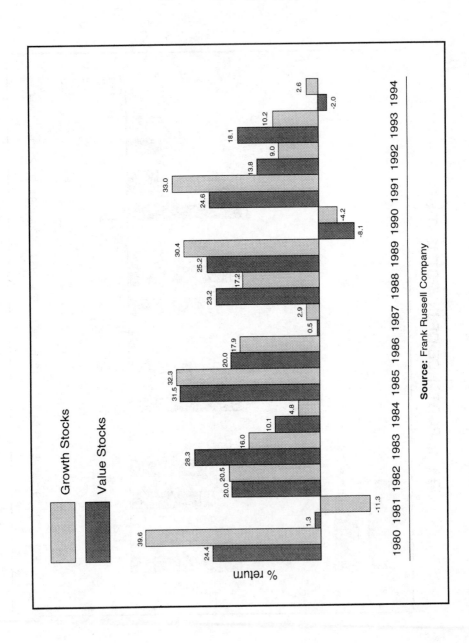

partment rules that date back to when few plans gave their investors much choice—hence disclosure wasn't very important. As a result, the printed information available on private funds is much sketchier, though the situation is improving.

Here's where to find data on your funds:

THE PROSPECTUS (MUTUAL FUNDS ONLY)

This is a legal document written by lawyers for lawyers, and it reads like it. Its main purpose isn't really to impart knowledge, but rather to protect the fund's sponsor from being sued for not disclosing enough. Hence the documents tend to say everything, which is often a lawyer's way of saying nothing.

Buried in this mess, however, is some useful information. In the first two pages of the prospectus is a table that details all the fund's expenses, expressed as a percentage of the money you've invested. The table includes the money manager's fee, the administrative expenses, and any marketing or sales charges. Look closely at the bottom line. That's the percentage of your nest egg you're turning over each year to the money-management firm for the privilege of investing with them.

The expense table is followed by a "per-share data" table of the fund's past record (assuming it has a past). Pay close attention to the line titled "Net investment income." This is the fund's yield. A yield over 3% is an indication of a relatively low-risk stock fund. It means either that the fund owns a lot of high-dividend stocks (typical of a value fund) or that it owns a few bonds; either way, that makes it safer than the average growth fund. A yield under 1% suggests a fund with a growth orientation.

Also near the front are the most useful text sections. They have titles like "Investment Objective," "Investment

Policies," "Investment Restrictions," and so on. They describe the fund's investment philosophy and goals. Often these passages are lucid and helpful and may even explicitly say that the fund subscribes to a growth or value investing style. Often they are obscure or overly general, which means that either (1) the lawyers drafting the prospectus didn't know the fund's investment approach; (2) they knew it but didn't care to make it clear to the shareholders; or (3) the fund has no investment philosophy. None is a good sign for 401(k) investors. If you can't figure out from these passages what the fund's approach really is, ask your benefits administrator or the fund group's hot line to shed some light.

MORNINGSTAR AND VALUE LINE (MUTUAL FUNDS ONLY)

These are the two main competitors in the business of researching mutual funds for consumers. Each publishes and continually updates a reference volume—called *Morningstar Mutual Funds* and *Value Line Mutual Fund Survey*—covering thousands of funds. Their research is packed with numerical data, along with a verbal review from one of the firm's analysts. Pay particular attention to the "style analysis box," which places each fund along a spectrum between growth and value on the one hand and big stocks and small stocks on the other. Also note the ratings of the fund's risk and return, which tell you how the fund stacked up against other funds in the same category. Finally, check the fund's year-by-year returns in relation to its peer group and market indexes (Morningstar goes back 10 years, Value Line goes back 15). That will give you an idea of the range of returns—good and bad—that the fund has produced in the past.

You can find one or both companies' volumes in major

public libraries. Too bad there is no comparable tool for plans that use private investment funds.

DAILY NEWSPAPERS (MUTUAL FUNDS ONLY)

Most major daily papers, as well as the *Wall Street Journal*, carry daily listings of mutual funds, detailing the previous day's rise or fall in share value (sometimes referred to as **net asset value**, or **NAV**). The better papers, including the *Journal*, also give you updated longer-term returns. You can follow your funds this way if you choose, but paying close attention to daily returns is not a useful activity for your 401(k) funds. It could even be dangerous if you get caught up in the market's day-to-day emotion and make a shortsighted move.

COMPANY DOCUMENTATION (ALL PLANS)

Unless your company is unusually tight-lipped, it will make an effort to fill you in on the investments in its plan. But these efforts vary widely from company to company and depend on how much information they think their employees can process; how queasy they are about seeming to give advice that can later be held against them; and how much help they get from the money-management firm or record keepers they've hired for the plan.

In the best case, your company's material will spell out the funds' investment style and size preferences, past performance, current dividend yield, and expenses, even if doing so repeats what's in a mutual fund prospectus. (Many companies wisely don't assume that employees get very far with the official prospectus.) Any good company material will

111

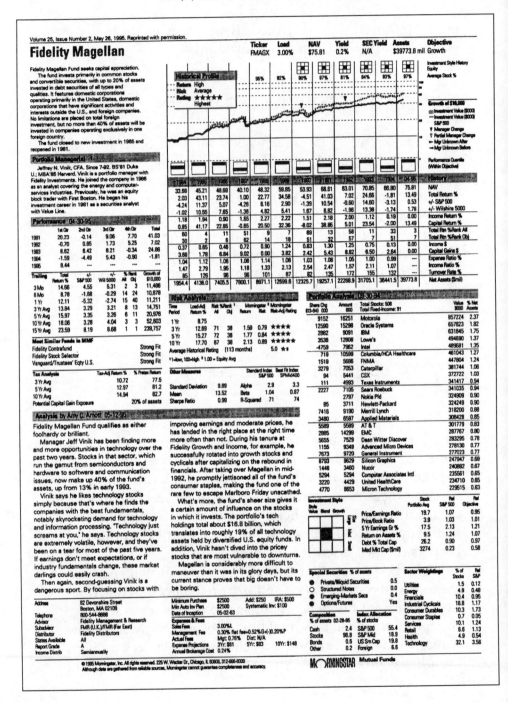

Volume 25, Issue Number 2, May 26, 1995. Reprinted with permission.

Fidelity Magellan

	Ticker	Load	NAV	Yield	SEC Yield	Assets	Objective
	FMAGX	3.00%	$75.81	0.2%	N/A	$39773.8 mil	Growth

Fidelity Magellan Fund seeks capital appreciation.

The fund invests primarily in common stocks and convertible securities, with up to 20% of assets invested in debt securities of all types and qualities. It features domestic corporations operating primarily in the United States, domestic corporations that have significant activities and interests outside the U.S., and foreign companies. No limitations are placed on total foreign investment, but no more than 40% of assets will be invested in companies operating exclusively in one foreign country.

The fund closed to new investment in 1966 and reopened in 1981.

Portfolio Manager(s)

Jeffrey N. Vinik, CFA. Since 7-92. BS'81 Duke U.; MBA'85 Harvard. Vinik is a portfolio manager with Fidelity Investments. He joined the company in 1986 as an analyst covering the energy and computer-services industries. Previously, he was an equity block trader with First Boston. He began his investment career in 1981 as a securities analyst with Value Line.

Performance 04-30-95

	1st Qtr	2nd Qtr	3rd Qtr	4th Qtr	Total
1991	20.23	-0.14	9.05	7.70	41.03
1992	-0.70	0.85	1.73	5.25	7.02
1993	8.62	6.42	8.21	-0.34	24.66
1994	-1.59	-4.49	5.43	-0.90	-1.81
1995	8.44	—	—	—	—

Trailing	Total Return %	+/- S&P 500	+/- Wil 5000	%Rank All	%Rank Obj	Growth of $10,000
3 Mo	14.66	4.55	5.31	2	3	11,466
6 Mo	8.78	-1.68	-0.29	14	24	10,878
1 Yr	12.11	-5.32	-2.74	15	40	11,211
3 Yr Avg	13.84	3.29	3.21	8	13	14,751
5 Yr Avg	15.97	3.35	3.26	6	11	20,976
10 Yr Avg	18.06	3.28	4.04	3	3	52,803
15 Yr Avg	23.59	8.19	8.68	1	1	239,757

Meet Similar Funds in MMF

Fidelity Contrafund	Strong Fit
Fidelity Stock Selector	Strong Fit
Vanguard/Trustees' Eqty U.S.	Strong Fit

Tax Analysis

	Tax-Adj Return %	% Pretax Return
3 Yr Avg	10.72	77.5
5 Yr Avg	12.97	81.2
10 Yr Avg	14.94	82.7
Potential Capital Gain Exposure		20% of assets

Analysis by Amy C. Arnott 05-12-95

Fidelity Magellan Fund qualifies as either foolhardy or brilliant.

Manager Jeff Vinik has been finding more and more opportunities in technology over the past two years. Stocks in that sector, which run the gamut from semiconductors and hardware to software and communication issues, now make up 40% of the fund's assets, up from 13% in early 1993.

Vinik says he likes technology stocks simply because that's where he finds the companies with the best fundamentals, notably skyrocketing demand for technology and information processing. "Technology just screams at you," he says. Technology stocks are extremely volatile, however, and they've been on a tear for most of the past five years. If earnings don't meet expectations, or if industry fundamentals change, these market darlings could easily crash.

Then again, second-guessing Vinik is a dangerous sport. By focusing on stocks with improving earnings and moderate prices, he has landed in the right place at the right time more often than not. During his tenure at Fidelity Growth and Income, for example, he successfully rotated into growth stocks and cyclicals after capitalizing on the rebound in financials. After taking over Magellan in mid-1992, he promptly jettisoned all of the fund's consumer staples, making the fund one of the rare few to escape Marlboro Friday unscathed.

What's more, the fund's sheer size gives it a certain amount of influence on the stocks in which it invests. The portfolio's tech holdings total about $16.8 billion, which translates into roughly 19% of all technology assets held by diversified U.S. equity funds. In addition, Vinik hasn't dived into the pricey stocks that are most vulnerable to downturns. Magellan is considerably more difficult to maneuver than it was in its glory days, but its current stance proves that big doesn't have to be boring.

Address	82 Devonshire Street Boston, MA 02109
Telephone	800-544-8888
Advisor	Fidelity Management & Research
Subadvisor	FMR (U.K.)/FMR (Far East)
Distributor	Fidelity Distributors
States Available	All
Report Grade	A
Income Distrib	Semiannually

Minimum Purchase	$2500	Add: $250	IRA: $500
Min Auto Inv Plan	$2500	Systematic Inv: $100	
Date of Inception	05-02-63		

Expenses & Fees

Sales Fees	3.00%L
Management Fee	0.30% flat fee+0.52%G+(-)0.20%P
Actual Fees	Mgt: 0.76% Dist: N/A
Expense Projections	3Yr: $81 5Yr: $83 10Yr: $148
Annual Brokerage Cost	0.24%

Historical Profile

Return: High
Risk: Average
Rating: ★★★★ Highest

Investment Style History — Equity — Average Stock %

95%	92%	90%	97%	81%	84%	80%	97%

Growth of $10,000 — Investment Value ($000) — Investment Value ($000) S&P 500 — Manager Change — Partial Manager Change — Mgr Unknown After — Mgr Unknown Before

Performance Quartile (Within Objective)

History

	1984	1985	1986	1987	1988	1989	1990	1991	1992	1993	1994	04-95	
NAV	33.69	45.21	48.69	40.10	48.32	58.85	53.93	68.61	63.01	70.85	66.80	75.81	NAV
Total Return %	2.03	43.11	23.74	1.00	22.77	34.58	-4.51	41.03	7.02	24.66	-1.81	13.49	Total Return %
	-4.24	11.37	5.07	-4.26	6.16	2.90	-1.39	10.54	-0.50	14.60	-3.13	0.53	+/- S&P 500
	-1.02	10.55	7.85	-1.36	4.82	5.41	1.67	8.82	-1.96	13.38	-1.74	1.78	+/- Wilshire 5000
	1.18	1.94	0.90	1.65	2.27	2.22	1.51	2.18	2.00	1.12	0.19	0.00	Income Return %
	0.85	41.17	22.85	-0.85	20.50	32.36	-6.02	38.85	5.01	23.54	-2.00	13.49	Capital Return %
	60	4	11	51	9	7	69	13	58	11	33	3	Total Rtn %Rank All
	30	2	8	62	14	18	51	32	57	7	51	7	Total Rtn %Rank Obj
	0.37	0.65	0.46	0.72	0.90	1.24	0.83	1.30	1.25	0.75	0.13	0.00	Income $
	3.68	1.78	6.84	9.02	0.00	3.82	2.42	5.43	8.82	6.50	2.64	0.00	Capital Gains $
	1.04	1.12	1.08	1.08	1.14	1.06	1.03	1.06	1.05	1.00	0.99	—	Expense Ratio %
	1.47	2.79	1.95	1.18	1.33	2.13	2.54	2.47	1.57	2.11	1.07	—	Income Ratio %
	85	126	96	96	101	87	82	135	172	155	132	—	Turnover Rate %
Net Assets ($mil)	1954.4	4136.0	7405.5	7800.1	8971.1	12699.6	12325.7	19257.1	22268.9	31705.1	36441.5	39773.8	Net Assets ($mil)

Risk Analysis

Time Period	Load-Adj Return %	Risk %Rank All	Risk %Rank Obj	Morningstar Return	Morningstar Risk	Morningstar Risk-Adj Rating
1 Yr	8.75					
3 Yr	12.69	71	38	1.58	0.79	★★★★
5 Yr	15.27	72	38	1.77	0.84	★★★★
10 Yr	17.70	67	38	2.13	0.89	★★★★
Average Historical Rating	(113 months)				5.0	★s

[1] = low, 100 = high [2] 1.00 = Equity Avg

Other Measures

	Standard Index S&P 500	Best Fit Index SPMid400
Standard Deviation	9.89	
Mean	13.52	
Sharpe Ratio	0.99	
Alpha	2.9	3.3
Beta	1.04	0.87
R-Squared	71	74

Portfolio Analysis 03-31-95

Total Stocks: 508				Value $000	% Net Assets
Total Fixed-Income: 91					
Share Chg (03-94)	Amount 000				
9152	16251	Motorola		857224	2.37
12590	15298	Oracle Systems		657823	1.82
2882	9091	IBM		631845	1.75
3536	12808	Lowe's		494690	1.37
-4759	7982	Intel		489681	1.35
719	10599	Columbia/HCA Healthcare		461043	1.27
1519	5686	FNMA		447804	1.24
3279	7053	Caterpillar		381744	1.06
94	5441	CSX		372272	1.03
111	4993	Texas Instruments		341417	0.94
2227	7105	Sears Roebuck		341035	0.94
	2797	Nokia Pfd		324909	0.90
85	3711	Hewlett-Packard		324249	0.90
7416	9190	Merrill Lynch		318200	0.88
3480	6587	Applied Materials		308428	0.85
5589	5589	AT&T		301779	0.83
2985	14299	EMC		287767	0.80
5655	7529	Dean Witter Discover		283295	0.78
1155	9348	Advanced Micro Devices		278130	0.77
7673	9720	General Instrument		277023	0.77
8793	9629	Silicon Graphics		247947	0.69
1446	3460	Nucor		240882	0.67
5294	5294	Computer Associates Intl		235561	0.65
3220	4429	United HealthCare		234710	0.65
4770	8653	Micron Technology		229515	0.63

Investment Style

Style Value Blend Growth		Stock Portfolio Avg	Rel S&P 500	Rel Objective
Price/Earnings Ratio		19.7	1.07	0.95
Price/Book Ratio		3.9	1.03	1.01
5 Yr Earnings Gr %		17.5	2.13	1.21
Return on Assets %		9.5	1.24	1.07
Debt % Total Cap		26.2	0.90	0.97
Med Mkt Cap ($mil)		3274	0.23	0.58

Special Securities % of assets

● Private/Illiquid Securities	0.5
○ Structured Notes	0.0
● Emerging-Markets Secs	0.4
● Options/Futures	Yes

Composition

% of assets 02-28-95	
Cash	2.4
Stocks	96.8
Bonds	0.6
Other	0.2

Index Allocation

% of stocks	
S&P 500	55.4
S&P Mid	18.9
US Sm Cap	19.8
Foreign	6.6

Sector Weightings

	% of Stocks	Rel S&P
Utilities	1.5	0.12
Energy	4.9	0.48
Financials	10.4	0.95
Industrial Cyclicals	16.8	1.17
Consumer Durables	10.3	1.73
Consumer Staples	0.7	0.05
Services	10.1	1.24
Retail	6.6	1.13
Health	4.9	0.54
Technology	32.1	3.56

MORNINGSTAR Mutual Funds

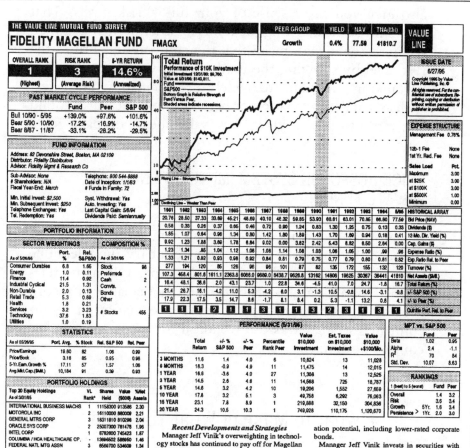

THE VALUE LINE MUTUAL FUND SURVEY

FIDELITY MAGELLAN FUND FMAGX

PEER GROUP	YIELD	NAV	TNA(Mil)
Growth	0.4%	77.50	41810.7

VALUE LINE

OVERALL RANK	RISK RANK	5-YR RETURN
1 (Highest)	3 (Average Risk)	14.6% (Annualized)

PAST MARKET CYCLE PERFORMANCE

	Fund	Peer	S&P 500
Bull 10/90 - 5/95	+139.0%	+97.6%	+101.6%
Bear 5/90 - 10/90	-17.2%	-16.9%	-14.7%
Bear 8/87 - 11/87	-33.1%	-28.2%	-29.5%

FUND INFORMATION

Address: 82 Devonshire Street, Boston, MA 02109
Distributor: Fidelity Distributors
Advisor: Fidelity Mgmt & Research Co

Sub-Advisor: None
Shareholders: N/A
Fiscal Year-End: March
Telephone: 800 544-8888
Date of Inception: 1/1/63
Funds in Family: 72

Min. Initial Invest: $2,500
Min. Subsequent Invest: $250
Telephone Exchanges: Yes
Tel. Redemption: Yes
Syst. Withdrawal: Yes
Auto. Investing: Yes
Last Capital Gain: 5/6/94
Dividends Paid: Semiannually

PORTFOLIO INFORMATION

SECTOR WEIGHTINGS

As of 5/26/95	Port. %	Rel. S&P500
Consumer Durables	6.8	1.65
Energy	1.0	0.11
Finance	11.4	0.92
Industrial Cyclical	21.5	1.31
Non-Durable	2.0	0.13
Retail Trade	5.3	0.89
Health	1.8	0.21
Services	3.2	3.23
Technology	37.6	1.83
Utilities	1.0	0.19

COMPOSITION %

As of 3/31/95	
Stock	96
Preferreds	-
Cash	2
Convts.	-
Bonds	1
Other	-
# Stocks	455

STATISTICS

As of 05/26/95	Port. Avg.	% Stock	Rel. S&P 500	Rel. Peer
Price/Earnings	19.80	82	1.06	0.99
Price/Book	3.16	85	0.95	0.98
5-Yr.Earn.Growth %	17.11	57	1.57	1.06
Avg.Mkt.Cap.($Mil.)	10,184	91	0.39	0.93

PORTFOLIO HOLDINGS

Top 20 Equity Holdings As of 3/31/95	VL Rank*	Shares Held (000s)	Value ($000)	%Net Assets
INTERNATIONAL BUSINESS MACHS	1	11158300	913586	2.30
MOTOROLA INC	2	16110000	880009	2.21
GENERAL MTRS CORP	3	1831181 0 810296		2.04
ORACLE SYS CORP	2	25007300	781478	1.96
INTEL CORP	1	8782600	745423	1.87
COLUMBIA / HCA HEALTHCARE CP.	-	13696502	588950	1.48
FEDERAL NATL MTG ASSN	3	6560700	534609	1.34
CSX CORP	2	6672800	525483	1.32
HEWLETT PACKARD CO	1	4214400	507306	1.27
MICRON TECHNOLOGY INC	1	6564300	496887	1.25
NOKIA AB FREE SHARES	1	3154500	480244	1.16
LOWES COS INC	3	12810100	441948	1.11
TEXAS INSTRS INC	1	4974000	440199	1.11
COMPUTER ASSOCIATE INTL INC	1	7317200	434459	1.09
CATERPILLAR INC	1	7660300	426104	1.07
APPLIED MATLS INC	1	7729100	426067	1.07
COMPAQ COMPUTER CORP	2	12053200	415835	1.04
CONRAIL INC	2	7382500	414343	1.04
MERRILL LYNCH & CO INC	3	9395299	400475	1.01
DIGITAL EQUIP CORP	1	10027000	379773	0.95

*Latest available Timeliness ™ rank from Value Line Investment Survey.

PORT. MGR.	%RATING
Jeff Vinik 7/92	2.4

TAX STATUS 3/31/92
Unrealized Apprec. % ... 18

Style/Perf. Quintile	
Large Cap.	2
Small Cap.	

DIVIDENDS PAID

Year	1st Q	2nd Q	3rd Q	4th Q
1991	--	0.53	--	0.77
1992	--	0.21	--	1.04
1993	--	0.26	--	0.49
1994	--	0.13	--	--
1995				

Total Return
Performance of $10K Investment

EXPENSE STRUCTURE

Management Fee	0.78%
12b-1 Fee	None
1st Yr. Red. Fee	None
Sales Load	Pct.
Maximum	3.00
at $25K	3.00
at $100K	3.00
at $500K	1.00
Minimum	0.00

HISTORICAL ARRAY

	1981	1982	1983	1984	1985	1986	1987	1988	1989	1990	1991	1992	1993	1994	5/95	
	20.76	28.50	37.33	33.89	45.21	48.59	40.10	46.32	59.85	53.93	68.61	63.01	70.86	66.80	77.50	Bid Price (NAV)
	0.58	0.30	0.26	0.37	0.85	0.46	0.72	0.90	1.24	0.83	1.30	1.25	0.75	0.13	0.35	Dividends ($)
	1.85	1.07	0.64	0.06	1.34	0.80	1.42	1.80	1.89	1.43	1.70	1.60	0.94	0.16	0.41	12-Mo. Div. Yield (%)
	9.92	1.23	1.88	3.69	1.78	6.84	9.02	0.00	3.82	2.42	5.43	8.82	6.50	2.84	0.00	Cap. Gains ($)
	1.23	1.34	.85	1.04	1.12	1.08	1.08	1.14	1.08	1.03	1.06	1.05	1.00	.99	.96	Expense Ratio (%)
	1.33	1.21	0.82	0.93	0.98	0.92	0.84	0.81	0.79	0.75	0.77	0.79	0.80	0.81	0.82	Exp. Ratio Rel. to Peer
	277	194	120	85	126	96	96	101	87	82	135	172	155	132	120	Turnover (%)
	107.3	464.4	801.6	1611.1	2363.8	6086.0	9680.0	8438.7	9626.8	13162	14806	19625	30367	36441	41810	Net Assets ($Mil.)
	16.4	48.1	38.6	2.0	43.1	23.7	1.0	22.8	34.6	-4.5	41.0	7.0	24.7	-1.8	16.7	Total Return (%)
	21.4	26.7	16.1	-4.2	11.0	5.3	-4.2	6.0	3.1	-1.3	10.5	-0.8	14.6	-3.1	-0.8	+/- S&P 500 (%)
	17.9	22.3	17.5	3.5	14.7	8.6	-1.7	8.1	8.4	0.2	5.3	-1.1	13.2	0.8	4.1	+/- to Peer (%)
	1	1	1	2	1	1	3	1	1	3	2	3	1	3	1	Quintile Perf. Rel. to Peer

PERFORMANCE (5/31/95)

	Total Return	+/- % S&P 500	+/- % Peer	Percentile Rank Peer	Value $10,000 Investment	Est. Taxes on $10,000 Investment	Value $10,000 +$100/Mo.
3 MONTHS	11.6	1.4	4.0	6	10,824	13	11,028
6 MONTHS	18.3	-0.9	4.9	11	11,475	14	12,015
1 YEAR	16.6	-3.6	4.0	27	11,308	13	12,525
3 YEAR	14.5	2.6	4.6	11	14,568	725	18,787
5 YEAR	14.6	3.2	4.2	10	19,206	1,552	27,659
10 YEAR	17.8	3.2	5.1	3	49,758	6,292	76,063
15 YEAR	23.1	7.8	8.9	1	219,888	32,150	304,836
20 YEAR	24.3	10.5	10.3	1	748,928	110,175	1,120,670

MPT vs. S&P 500

	Fund	Peer
Beta	1.02	0.95
Alpha	2.4	-1.1
R²	70	84
Std. Dev.	10.07	8.63

RANKINGS

1 (best) to 5 (worst)	Fund	Peer
Overall	1.4	3.2
Risk	3.6	3.4
Growth	1.6	3.4
Persistence > 1Yr.	2.0	3.0

Recent Developments and Strategies

Manager Jeff Vinik's overweighting in technology stocks has continued to pay off for Magellan fund. The portfolio's weighting in this sector has been boosted—to more than 40% by the end of March—based on Vinik's belief that reasonable earnings valuations and rising domestic capital spending make the sector the most attractive by far. He has also doubled the weighting in financial stocks, including U.S. brokerage issues, over the last year, another positive catalyst. Cyclical stocks represent a large weighting in the fund as well; according to Vinik, auto and auto parts companies, railroads, and industrial equipment manufacturers' valuations do not take into account lower costs, higher productivity, and the potential for consistently strong profits.

Management Style

The fund seeks capital appreciation. It invests primarily in common stocks, and other securities convertible into common stocks, of U.S., multinational, and foreign companies of all sizes that are deemed to offer potential for growth. The fund can also invest in domestic and foreign debt securities that are believed to have capital appreci-

ation potential, including lower-rated corporate bonds.

Manager Jeff Vinik invests in securities with strong current earnings that he believes have excellent prospects for future earnings growth. He attempts to position the fund correctly for the next two to three years, rather than the next two or three months, and hence is not overly concerned with short-term market swings. He is supported in his efforts by Fidelity's extensive research capabilities.

Conclusion

As Vinik closes in on his third anniversary, skeptics have little to gloat about; the fund has added to its impressive track record. With the best research ideas that Fidelity can produce continuously funneled to a talented manager, the only uncertainty that will continue to dog the fund is Magellan's status as the largest—by far—mutual fund in the industry. Total assets now stand at over $40 billion, effectively forcing the fund to either expand the number of holdings, making it tougher to beat the market, or to concentrate its holdings as it did with technology, thus increasing risk.

also give you some sense of your funds' risk levels. That may simply mean listing the funds in order of their assumed riskiness, or it may mean that the company quantifies the risk level by showing the fund's worst year or quarter, or its ranking according to widely used statistical measures, such as standard deviation or beta. (If those measures sound like Urdu to you, review "Risky Business" on page 76.)

VOICE RESPONSE SYSTEM (MUTUAL FUNDS AND PRIVATE FUNDS)

If your plan's documentation leaves you short of information about your stock funds, you might try the telephone information system if your plan has one. Often the telephone reps are employees of the money manager or record keeper, and they may have access to information that your company decided was too technical for its own employee communications.

What to Make of What You Find

PAST PERFORMANCE

This is probably the most useful information you can get—and potentially the most misleading. That's because it's so tempting to make the elementary mistake of projecting past performance into the future. The fact is, no money manager stays on top forever, and simply homing in on the fund with the hottest performance increases the chance that you will buy it just as it peaks.

Instead of flashy gains, you want consistency and relative predictability. Ideally, your funds should perform slightly above average for their investment category and investment style. (You'll find year-by-year benchmark returns for four different investment styles in the charts on pages 107 and 108. Category averages are in the table on page 93.) A consistently laggard performance is not a good sign, for obvious reasons, but wildly superior returns year after year are suspicious, too. They could be a sign that the fund is taking excessive risks—an aggressive growth fund in growth-and-income clothing, for example. That sleight-of-hand can cause a fund to lead its category during bull markets, but in less hospitable markets, there is generally a price to pay.

RISK LEVEL

Some chance of principal loss is part of the bargain when you invest in your 401(k)'s stock funds. If you eliminate that, you eliminate your fund's potential for inflation-beating long-term gains. At the same time, though, you want to make sure the fund isn't prone to accidents that might cause you to come unglued from your long-term strategy. So take a look at the fund's risk measures compared with others of its type, and find out the fund's worst yearly return (or worst quarterly return, if available). Is it something you could sit through without losing your cool? If not, you might prefer an equity fund that follows a more stable investing approach.

EXPENSES

Drawing conclusions from a fund's past performance and risk can be ambiguous—sometimes a lower return in the past is preferable to a higher one, for example, if it means the fund was true to its style and investment category.

By contrast, there's no ambiguity when it comes to interpreting expenses. Lower is better. Every percentage point that your funds pay in money-management fees reduces your return by the same amount. This assumes, as is usually the case, that the money-management fees are subtracted from the fund's assets—that is, your assets. If your employer is picking up the tab, fund expenses are not your problem.

Customary expense levels vary with the category of fund. For example, internationals, which require more extensive research and impose higher administrative costs, charge higher fees than growth and income funds. And equity-index funds, which require no investment decisions from their managers, ought to be the lowest-cost equity funds of all. You can get an idea of whether your fees are close to the going rate by checking the table on page 117, which gives the averages for each category. If your funds' expenses are much higher than average, let your employer know that you know the expenses are high. The company's trustees, as fiduciaries, are responsible for assuring that the plan expenses are reasonable. You should insist that they take that responsibility to heart.

KEY POINTS

- Analyzing your plan's stock funds can help you understand why the funds perform as they do. And as plans continue to offer participants a greater number of stock fund options, you are increasingly likely to have to choose funds wisely.
- Much of a stock fund's performance can be explained by a combination of its investing style and by the size of the companies it invests in.
- If your plan's stock investment options are mutual funds, you'll find most of the information you'll need about them

WHAT'S A FAIR PRICE FOR YOUR FUNDS?

Stock Funds	Median Expense (% of assets)
Aggressive growth	1.75
Growth	1.39
Growth and income	1.23
Equity index	0.61
Equity income	1.30
Balanced	1.28
Asset allocation	1.46
International stock	1.64
Income Funds	
Corporate bond	0.95
U.S. government bond	1.04
Bond index	0.36
Money market	0.78

Source: Morningstar Inc., Chicago.

in the prospectus and in the research published in *Morningstar Mutual Funds* and *Value Line Mutual Fund Survey*.

- If your plan uses private funds, you will have to dig a little harder. If you can't find what you need to know in company descriptions of the investment options, call the plan's telephone service line (if it has one) or ask your benefits administrator for help.

CHAPTER 8

Oil on the Waters: Your 401(k)'s Bond Funds

If stocks funds are the leading players of your 401(k) plan, income funds are the supporting cast. They will rarely be the headline performers in your 401(k)—at least not for very long periods—and they almost certainly won't be the ones getting the ovations when you start counting your money at retirement. But if they weren't there, the show would be a lot more precarious.

The role of income funds is to balance the risk of your stock funds. The types of income funds found in 401(k)s—bond funds, money-markets, and guaranteed income contracts (GICs)—are all much less accident-prone than stocks. They are also, predictably, less likely to soar. Adding them to a portfolio of stock funds will probably lower your expected return somewhat, but they will lower the volatility of your portfolio even more.

Though income funds all add stability to a 401(k) portfolio, they differ dramatically from one another in the amount and types of risks they incur themselves. For this reason, we've divided our discussion of income funds into two parts. This chapter covers bond funds, by far the riskier incarnation of income fund, which are offered by slightly more than half of all 401(k)s. The following chapter discusses cash-equivalent income funds: money-markets and GICs.

The Case for Bond Funds

Anyone who owned bond funds through 1994 may think it odd that financial experts consider them a way to lower risk in your 401(k). But while it's true that bond funds occasionally have bad-hair days (or years), they don't suffer the precipitous drops that stocks do. Even in 1994, the bond market's worst calendar year since the early 1980s, most 401(k) bond funds lost 5% or less. And if you held on to bonds for three years running at any time going back to 1926, you wouldn't have lost as much as one percentage point.

Equally important, when bond investments do run into trouble, they tend to do so on a different schedule from the stock market. (As you will discover in Chapter 10, the scientific way to express this thought is to say that the **correlation** between the performance of stocks and bonds is low.) In 15 of the past 20 years when the S&P 500 lost money, long-term bonds *gained* an average of 5.5%.

Bond fund detractors point out that economic changes in recent decades—among them the fact that inflation has apparently taken up permanent residence in the economy—make bonds riskier than they have been for most of their history. They say that devoting a slice of your 401(k) to money funds or GICs can soften your stock market risk as much as bonds can without bonds' peccadilloes.

But this is a minority view. Most experts believe that the

bond market will adjust. If the economy continues to run a low-grade inflation fever, bond yields will rise to compensate investors—and, indeed, in recent years bond yields have retained a much higher margin over inflation than previously. The consensus thinking is that in the long run, bond funds figure not only to help diversify your 401(k) account, but also to give you a higher return than you'd get from cash investments.

How the Bond Markets Work

The bond market may generate fewer headlines than the stock market, but not because it generates fewer dollars. The U.S. bond market totals some $7 trillion dollars, making it about two and a half times the size of the domestic stock market. And in recent years the bond market has not exactly lacked for drama, either. As interest rates tumbled through the mid-1980s, long-term bonds returned more than 20% a year, exceeding the gains on stocks. They also had their share of reversals, 1994 being the most recent one.

A bond is a loan, an IOU from a corporation or from a government borrower like the Treasury or the Federal National Mortgage Association. It doesn't matter that the IOU may have passed through the hands of many other investors before you (or your 401(k) fund) bought it. You get paid interest according to the terms of the loan, just like the original owner. And like that owner, you want to be paid an interest rate that provides a decent return and compensates you for taking the risks of lending.

What risks? The first one that might come to mind is the chance that the borrower could get into financial difficulty and not be able to pay you back on schedule. This is called **credit risk**. To keep it under control, bond investors ana-

TYPICAL 401(k) BOND FUND CHOICES

Fund Type and Typical Investment	Risk Level (Standard Deviation)	Average Maturity	Yield	Annualized Total Return as of Mid-1995		
				One Year	Three Years	Five Years
Corporate bond: Bonds issued by solid domestic corporations	Medium to low (4.4)	8.2 years	6.3%	9.7%	7.3%	9.2%
U.S. government: Bonds issued by the U.S. Treasury or U.S. agencies	Medium to low (4.1)	7.2 years	5.7%	8.5%	5.9%	7.9%
Bond index: Strives to replicate the performance of bond market indicators	Medium to low (3.6)	8.5 years	7.0%	12.1%	7.3%	9.0%
Money-market funds: Short-term IOUs issued by high-grade corporations and the U.S. government	Very low (1.0)	51 days	5.4%	4.4%	3.6%	4.5%

Source: Morningstar Inc., Chicago.

lyze the financial strength of companies they lend to or else refer to research done by credit rating agencies like Moody's and Standard & Poor's. Both agencies assign letter grades to the borrowers they examine, based on the borrower's perceived financial strength. Though the exact grammar differs slightly from one rating company to another, a top rating (triple A) from either company means that it's almost inconceivable that the issuer won't come through. Federal government issues, for example, are automatically triple-A because Washington can always pay off its debt simply by raising taxes. Triple-B is the lowest so-called investment grade you can buy; it's the rating given to companies that are less than sure things but still unlikely to become deadbeats.

Why would anyone buy anything but triple-A debt? Because you get rewarded for doing so. The old risk vs. return equation applies here as well: the higher the credit risk you take on, the higher the interest rate you get paid. As of late 1997, for example, the typical low-quality corporate bond yielded about 1.65 percentage points more than the typical high-quality version.

The Interest Rate Seesaw

The other thing that can go wrong in the bond market— and it went drastically wrong in 1994—is that the level of interest rates in the economy can go up. There's a kind of a Newtonian law in the bond market: When interest rates go up, bond prices go down; when interest rates go down, bond prices go up. For example, if interest rates were to rise one percentage point tomorrow, the market price of three-year Treasuries would drop 3%. If rates declined by a point, the price of three-year Treasuries would rise 3%.

This inverse relationship between bond prices and yields

BOND RATING SYSTEMS

Standard & Poor's	Moody's	Meaning
AAA	Aaa	The highest credit quality, assigned to relatively few blue-chip corporations and to issues of the U.S. government
AA	Aa	High-quality credit; indicates the issuer is extremely unlikely to fail to pay interest or repay principal
A	A	Indicates a financially solid issuer, though somewhat more susceptible to trouble in adverse economic conditions
BBB	Baa	The lowest investment grade; indicates adequate credit quality but less ability to weather unexpected misfortune
BB or below	Ba or below	Indicates less than reliable ability to repay principal and interest as promised

confuses a lot of 401(k) investors. After all, it seems, it ought to be good for a lender if interest rates go up. That means you get paid more for lending the same amount of money.

True, but higher rates are nothing but trouble if you've *already* made a loan, which is what you've done if you own a bond. The interest rate on an existing bond is fixed for the bond's entire term, so it does you no good if the interest rate on new bonds goes higher. Your bond will continue to pay the same rate it always did. Inevitably, that makes it less valuable to other investors in the income market.

For example, suppose you buy a bond for $1,000 that pays 7%—or $70 a year. Then interest rates go up and one year later borrowers are paying 8% on their bonds, or $80 per $1,000 borrowed. Since your old bond still pays only $70, no investors in their right mind would buy it from you for $1,000 when for the same price they could get a new bond paying $80. To sell the bond at all, you'd have to sell at a loss.

Now try the reverse case. Say that interest rates went down to 6%—or $60 per $1,000 invested. Your $70 of annual income is now worth more than $1,000 to a bond buyer. So if you wanted to sell your bond at that point, you'd make a capital gain.

If you follow that logic, you're ready now for the corollary to the First Law of the Income Market: The farther off the maturity of the bond, the more pronounced its reaction to any move in rates. So the same one-percentage-point shift in rates that moves the prices of three-year Treasuries by 3% might bounce 10-year bonds by 7% and 30-year Treasuries by 11%. The reason ought to be clear: A bond that's stuck paying a below market interest rate for 30 years is a much bigger liability than one that pays the low rate for only three. Accordingly, the price of the 30-year bond falls farther. Again, the reverse is true if rates fall. A bond paying above market interest rates for 30 years is a bigger prize than one that carries its high rates for just three years.

Given the longer bonds' steeper risks, why would anyone bother owning them? You guessed it: higher yields. The yield on 10-year U.S. Treasury bonds typically ranges from a fraction of a percentage point to more than two points higher than on one-year Treasuries; the yield on 30-year Treasuries is typically a fraction of a percentage point higher still. (Occasionally, custom stands on its head and shorter-term bonds have higher yields; but this phenomenon, which often precedes an economic recession, tends to be short-lived.)

BOND PRICE WORKSHEET

How Far Bond Prices Will Fall If Interest Rates Rise

Maturity (Years)

Interest Rate Increase	1	3	7	10	20	30
0.50%	−0.5%	−1.3%	−2.7%	−3.6%	−5.3%	−6.2%
1.00%	−0.9%	−2.6%	−5.4%	−6.9%	−10.3%	−11.9%
1.50%	−1.4%	−3.9%	−7.9%	−10.2%	−14.8%	−17.0%
2.00%	−1.9%	−5.2%	−10.4%	−13.3%	−19.1%	−21.6%
2.50%	−2.3%	−6.4%	−12.8%	−16.3%	−23.0%	−25.8%

How Far Bond Prices Will Rise If Interest Rates Fall

Maturity (Years)

Interest Rate Decline	1	3	7	10	20	30
−0.50%	0.5%	1.4%	2.8%	3.7%	5.8%	6.9%
−1.00%	1.0%	2.7%	5.7%	7.6%	12.0%	14.6%
−1.50%	1.4%	4.1%	8.8%	11.7%	18.8%	23.2%
−2.00%	1.9%	5.6%	11.9%	16.0%	26.2%	32.7%
−2.50%	2.4%	7.0%	15.1%	20.4%	34.2%	43.5%

Assumptions: All bonds pay an interest rate of 6.5%

125

Remember, too, that price fluctuations are only one component of a bond's total return. The interest payments you receive count for far more. A sharp rise in rates could drop the price of a bond far enough to give you a negative total return for a year or more. But over a full decade, even a disastrous decade such as 1971 to 1981, when long-term interest rates went from 6% to more than 13%, the buildup of continual, steady interest payments more than offset the price decline. Despite ending the period with U.S. interest rates at an all-time peak, bond investors finished the decade 32% ahead of where they started, an annual total return of 2.8%.

Of Interest Rates, Inflation, and Bond Market Ghouls

Because of the Newtonian law of bond prices (prices and interest rates move in oppositve directions), bond investors spend a good deal of their time wondering about the direction of interest rates. If you could consistently tell where rates were going to be next week or next month, you would soon be very wealthy, not to mention the most employable person on Wall Street. Alas, no mortal has ever demonstrated any such ability.

That doesn't stop bond investors from poring over any economic statistic that offers any hint as to the direction of rates. Interest rates move in a cycle related to the business cycle: in a strong economy, expanding businesses and confident consumers increase the demand for loans, driving up interest rates. Bond prices go down. When the economy tips into recession, however, loan demand falls off and interest rates drop. Bond prices go up.

As a result, bond investors tend to be cheered by economic news that depresses everyone else—rising unemployment, declining home sales, slowing economic growth—and to be depressed by news that delights everyone else, like higher consumer confidence and healthy economic growth. Because of their perverse reaction to economic news, bond investors are jokingly referred to as "ghouls."

About the only feeling the bond ghouls share with right-thinking folk is an aversion to inflation. Inflation erodes the value of a bond's fixed-interest payments as well as its principal. Inflation also inexorably lifts interest rates, as lenders demand higher interest rates to offset the likelihood that they will be repaid in depreciated dollars. Inflation, however, tends to be more of a danger when the economy is strong than when it's weak. So bond investor's loathing for inflation only reinforces their preference for grim economic news—and leaves ordinary people more convinced than ever that Wall Street doesn't operate by the same rules as the rest of us.

Bond Funds

For the most part, a bond fund simply assumes the character of the bonds it owns. If they collectively go up or down in price, so does the share value or unit value of the bond fund. Likewise, the fund's yield reflects the average yield of all the bonds in the portfolio (minus the fund's expenses). Every fund also has a maturity—simply, the average maturity of all the bonds in the portfolio. For example, if the fund had half its money in bonds that matured in two years and half in bonds maturing in four years, the fund's overall maturity would be three years. As with individual bonds, the longer a fund's average maturity, the more sensitive its price will be to changes in interest rates.

A fund manager can vary the average maturity by trading long-term bonds for short-term or vice versa, but most funds keep within a range defined by the fund's investment policy. **Short-term bond funds** tend to keep their average maturity at less than three years; **intermediate-term funds** aim for the three-to-10-year middle ground; and **long-term funds** inhabit the high-interest-rate wilderness out beyond 10 years. Most 401(k) bond funds are of the intermediate variety.

Choosing Bond Funds

To get information about your bond funds, you should tap the same sources you did to learn about stock funds. Bond mutual funds issue prospectuses that are identical to stock fund prospectuses in format (and in the deadliness of their prose, unfortunately). *Morningstar Mutual Funds* and *Value Line Mutual Fund Survey* cover publicly sold bond mutual funds as well as stock funds. And as with stock funds, if your bond funds are private investment funds rather than mutual funds, you will have to scrape for such dog ends of information as your company and your plan's administrator and money manager see fit to disclose.

Some important questions to get answered:

For corporate bond funds, check the fund's credit quality. Government funds, by definition, will have triple-A credit ratings, but funds identified only as corporate or general bond funds may shoulder considerable credit risk. Check your prospectus or benefits administrator to make sure the fund's average credit rating is at least triple B, the minimum for so-called investment grade. While many lower-grade funds (also known as **junk funds**) have impressive long-term returns, they perform miserably in recessions. If a majority of your 401(k) is already in stock funds, you don't need another investment that rises and falls in sympathy with the economy.

Ask for the fund's average maturity or, better yet, its duration. Interest rate fluctuations are the main risk you will face in your bond fund investments. So it's important to find out your fund's policy on the maturity of its bonds. Then check that against the table on page 125 to get a sense of how much risk you face.

An even more precise measure of a bond's interest rate sensitivity is a statistic known as **duration**. It's like maturity, but it takes into account other factors that also affect a bond fund's interest rate jumpiness, such as the level of interest payments it makes. Duration gives you an easy, shorthand way to estimate the shift in price you can expect from a bond fund if interest rates change. Just multiply the duration by the expected change in rates. For example, a bond fund with a duration of seven years would rise about 7% in price if interest rates fell 1% percent. If they fell 2%, the price would jump about 14%.

Not every 401(k) plan can tell you the duration of the bond funds it offers. But *Morningstar* and *Value Line* calculate the data for the bond funds they track. Even if your plan doesn't use mutual funds, it's worth asking your benefits administrator.

Expenses are even more important. Because bonds tend to react in unison to interest rate moves, there is little opportunity for a bond fund manager to achieve the kind of bravura performance that the most successful stock fund managers achieve. For example, as of late 1997, the number one intermediate-term government bond mutual fund of the previous five years outperformed the number 20 fund by only three percentage points a year. By contrast, the top-ranked agressive growth mutual fund (this is a kind of stock fund, remember) had a 10-point annual advantage over the 20th-ranked fund of its type.

Most angling for advantage among bond fund managers consists of making minor bets on the direction of interest rates. For example, if the manager anticipates a decline in interest rates, she may load up on bonds at the long end of her approved range, so that the fund gets the biggest rise if she's right. Likewise, if she anticipates a rise in rates, she may shorten up to minimize the price damage. In practice, however, she is not likely to be right often enough to overcome the costs of trading. Bond market timing is as futile as stock market timing. Indeed, many of the market's shrewdest investors were caught flat-footed by 1994's sudden interest rate hike.

All that makes the case for index investing even stronger in the bond market than in the stock market. Indeed, of more than 1,400 bond funds tracked by Morningstar, only 142 had higher returns over the five years through late 1997 than the Lehman Brothers Aggregate Bond Index, a widely followed broad index of the bond market. Unfortunately, **bond index funds** are still fairly rare in 401(k) plans, though the concept is catching on. If your plan doesn't offer an index fund, at least make sure that the fund you are offered does not charge annual fees in excess of about 0.75%. Since it is so difficult for a manager to get ahead by savvy bond picking, funds that keep expenses low often have an insurmountable advantage over other funds.

KEY POINTS

- Bond funds ought to play a supporting role in your 401(k). They siphon risk out of an all-stock portfolio, helping to smooth out the ups and downs of investing.
- Though the bond market has been riskier in recent decades than it had been previously, a bond fund is still considerably less likely to crash than a stock fund.
- Bonds face two major drawbacks: credit risk—the chance that your borrower won't pay up—and interest rate risk, the chance that interest rates will go up and the value of your fund will go down.
- To gauge those risks in your 401(k)'s bond funds, find out their average credit rating from the major rating organizations, such as Moody's and Standard & Poor's. Also learn your funds' duration, the most reliable measure of interest rate risk.
- If your plan offers a low–expense bond index fund, take it.

CHAPTER 9

Safety First:
Your Capital
Preservation Funds

If the previous chapters left you weary with their discussions of risk and the multiplicity of ways you can lose money (even if temporarily) in your stock and bond funds, this chapter should bring you peace. Virtually every 401(k) includes at least one "capital preservation" option—an investment so low in principal risk that even the most conservative employees don't mind investing in it. How safe are they? There has never been a year in which the average 401(k) capital preservation fund came close to losing money. In fact, few 401(k) investors have had so much as a down day in such investments. (Although it can happen, as we'll discuss later on.)

The two most widely used are money-market funds and guaranteed investment contracts (GICs). The chief danger with them is that 401(k) investors can grow too fond of their safety. According to a study by benefits consultant Foster Higgins, GICs (pronounced with a hard *g*, as in "gift") draw an average of 43% of participants' total investments in the plans in which they're offered. That makes them easily the most widely used investment option. (All equity funds together equal only 31%.) Even in plans that include seven options or more, GICs' share is 38%.

Keeping that much money in your capital preservation fund rarely makes sense. Neither GICs nor money-markets are designed to be the core of a long-term 401(k) strategy. They should be used only when a need for short-term safety outweighs your long-term requirement for inflation-beating returns. Examples: when you are closing in on the point at which you will need to spend the money in your plan or when you need to park your money temporarily between investment options.

In the long run, however, making a big, permanent commitment to your capital preservation funds is the opposite of safe. Very little is certain in the financial markets, but the thing that comes closest is that inflation will grind away at the relatively low returns that capital preservation funds produce. The nub of a return that's left won't buy you much of a retirement.

One more point about safety: Both GICs and money-markets have lived up to their ultrasafe billing. But they are not totally free of principal risk. Things can go wrong, and in some conceivable circumstances—very nearly realized in some plans in this decade—you could lose money in them. Low risk, even very low risk, is not the same as no risk.

Money-Market Funds

Money funds invest in cash-equivalent securities: extremely short-term IOUs from the government, banks, and top-quality corporations. The Securities and Exchange Commission (SEC) orders that a money fund's average maturity can be no longer than 90 days, though in practice most funds keep their maturities between 40 and 75 days most of the time.

The funds are managed to maintain a constant share value of $1—in other words, never to lose (or gain) any principal. How can they do that? Part of the explanation is that the typical security in a money fund has such a short life span that its price changes hardly at all in response to interest rate fluctuations. (And special accounting rules allow money funds to accommodate what little price fluctuation does occur simply by raising or lowering the fund's yield.) Another reason is that the SEC requires funds to keep almost all their money in government securities or commercial paper that has been top rated by Moody's and Standard & Poor's. As a further safeguard, the fund's investments in commercial securities are diversified among scores of different issuers.

This triple set of checks and balances makes that $1 share value nearly as bulletproof as an Abrams tank. During the 25 years that money funds have been in business, only one true money fund (Community Bankers U.S. Government, in 1994) ever sank below the $1 level—and that fund's shareholders were institutions, not people. However, in the past six years a few dozen other funds have technically "broken the buck," as it's called. Fortunately, in every case the fund's management voluntarily stepped in and made up the losses out of its own pocket. The closest shave in a 401(k) plan took place in 1994, when a money fund look-alike in Atlantic Richfield's plan broke under the dollar barrier. That fund wasn't a true money-market, however, since it did not follow all the official safety precautions. (It called itself a "Money Market Plus" fund.) In any event, like other fund sponsors, the company stepped up and made good on the fund's losses, though it was not obliged to do so.

Money funds' high-quality, ultra-short-term IOUs give them a good deal of flexibility as well as safety. Because a fund manager can quickly convert such securities into cash, few employers restrict your ability to transfer your money into or out of your money fund (apart from restrictions that apply to all the funds in the plan, of course). That makes them particularly useful as a layover for money that you may be preparing to withdraw or transfer to another plan. That freedom isn't always available from guaranteed investment contracts, the other capital preservation fund found in 401(k)s.

Guaranteed Investment Contracts

Chances are good that your plan offers this option or something like it. Better than 60% of plans have GICs, making them the single most common investment choice. But chances are equally good that the name your plan has assigned to its GIC option bears no resemblance to "guaranteed investment contract." "Income fund," "stable principal fund," and "capital preservation fund" are all popular variations. Whatever your plan calls its GIC fund, however, the central investment is the guaranteed investment contract, an investment with a strong resemblance to a bank certificate of deposit, except that it is issued by an insurance company.

In the simplest version of a GIC, your plan negotiates an arrangement with an insurance company in which the insurer agrees to pay the plan a specific interest rate over a stated period, typically three to five years. (As with bonds, the longer the maturity, the higher the yield.) The plan hands the money over to the insurer, who invests it, hoping to earn a rate high enough to pay its obligation to the 401(k) and still turn a profit. Usually an employer will buy several GICs issued by different insurers—and participants in the plan get a share of the assembled GICs' total income—or it will hand over the money to an investment firm that manages a fund of GICs.

However the plan sets up its GIC fund, the investment has two big pluses for 401(k) investors. First, the value of your principal isn't affected by interest rate moves. That's because a GIC is essentially a contract between the plan and the insurance issuer, not a security that trades like a bond. Since there is no real market constantly setting a value for GICs, your plan values the GIC at a constant level. If you withdraw all your money from the GIC, you get back the principal you put into the fund, plus whatever interest you earned—just like a bank CD.

In addition, GICs typically pay considerably higher interest than money-market funds. In late 1997, for example, a typical three-year GIC paid about 6.5%; the typical money-market fund paid 5.2%. In fact, most of the time GIC interest rates are fairly close to the yields on intermediate-term government bond funds. So if your plan offers a GIC but no bond fund, you can simply substitute the GIC fund for the bond fund in your asset allocation.

GIC yields aren't always superior, however. When interest rates are rising, money fund yields will adjust much more quickly than GICs, as the money fund's manager reinvests the cash from its continually maturing securities at the higher rates. The rate on a GIC fund can climb only when a contract matures and the principal is ready for reinvestment or when the plan collects enough contributions from participants to buy a new contract at the new rate. Of course, GICs' slow turnover is an advantage when rates are falling: they pay the old, higher rates for a longer time than money-markets can.

An astute reader of previous chapters might notice that GICs break one cardinal rule of prudent investment. They're not diversified. The likelihood that any single GIC will pay off on its promise depends entirely on the financial

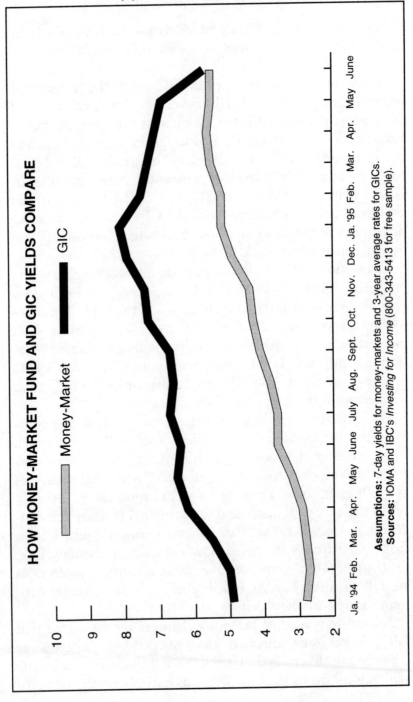

HOW MONEY-MARKET FUND AND GIC YIELDS COMPARE

Money-Market

GIC

Ja. '94 Feb. Mar. Apr. May June July Aug. Sept. Oct. Nov. Dec. Ja. '95 Feb. Mar. Apr. May June

Assumptions: 7-day yields for money-markets and 3-year average rates for GICs.
Sources: IOMA and IBC's *Investing for Income* (800-343-5413 for free sample).

health of the insurance company issuing the contract. Even if the plan directly owns GICs issued by half a dozen different insurers or owns shares in a fund that holds a score of GICs, the investment is still vulnerable to any setback that affects the insurance industry as a whole. No bond or money-market fund would concentrate its holdings in a single industry.

True, insurance companies are pretty conservative institutions by and large, but they can be brought down by unforeseen difficulties. That happened in 1991, when two insurers, Executive Life in California and Mutual Benefit Life in New Jersey, were both rendered insolvent by reverses on their other investments and were taken over by state regulators. Between them they had placed GICs in hundreds of 401(k) plans. As it turned out, regulators and other insurance companies worked out rescue plans that held losses to a minimum. In New Jersey, for example, plans owning Mutual Benefit GICs were given the option of cashing out immediately for about 60 cents on the dollar or holding on for several more years at a minimal interest rate and getting back all their principal. But that deal took more than two years to arrange, during which time the affected plans had limited access to their money and no idea what return, if any, they would get.

To counteract the credit risk of GICs, many plans have bought special disaster-resistant models. So-called separate account GICs are backed by a separate portfolio of high-quality bonds rather than by the insurance company's promise. So-called synthetic GICs were created out of portfolios of intermediate bonds (to approximate a GIC's yield), backed by an insurance company's promise to protect investors from interest rate risk on the portfolio. Thanks to these new products—and a generally higher level of financial strength among insurance companies—credit worries about GICs have faded. No doubt some as-yet-unknown risk will arise in the future and throw a scare into insurance companies again. But the chance that 401(k) participants will take a serious hit is probably quite small.

There is one other drawback to GIC investments in some plans: You often face restrictions on moving your money into and out of the fund. Some insurance companies may insist that 401(k) participants not be allowed to transfer money between their GIC and a money-market and possibly other income funds as well.

That's because in order to make a profit, the insurance company needs the cash flows into and out of the GIC to remain predictable. If 401(k) investors yank their money out of the GIC and into the money-market whenever interest rates go up—and back again whenever interest rates go down—any hope for predictable cash flow is gone. Other GIC fund managers accommodate transfers by keeping a certain amount of the fund invested in easily accessible cash investments such as Treasury bills. While that allows the fund to avoid imposing restrictions, it lowers the GIC fund's return since a certain portion of it must be invested in low-yielding bills rather than GICs.

Which makes better sense for the capital preservation portion of your 401(k)? Assuming your plan offers both options, you should probably go for the GIC, to take advantage of its higher yield. The only exception: The money-market fund is preferable if you plan to use the option only as a temporary parking place—say, between other investment options or in preparation for making a withdrawal—and your GIC option is subject to restrictions on transfers that would interfere with that use.

GIC funds are not risky investments by any means, but just for peace of mind, you may want to make sure that your plan takes precautions against credit risk. Find out from your benefits administrator whether the investments in your plan's GIC option are directed by your company or by an independent money manager. If the GICs are run in-house, check your company's policy regarding credit ratings. (Your company should invest only in GICs issued by insurers rated AA or better by Moody's or Standard & Poor's.) If your GIC option is a fund run by outside money managers, make sure it is well diversified. It's best if the fund has no more than 10% of its assets in any one issuer.

Key Points

- Money-market funds and guaranteed investment contracts are the only 401(k) investment options with almost (but not quite) zero principal risk.
- They make sense as temporary parking places for your money or as a kind of ballast to stabilize your portfolio against stock and bond market risk.
- Of the two options, money-market funds are more flexible and tend to reflect interest rate changes more quickly, while GIC funds generally have higher yields.
- If your plan doesn't have a bond fund, use the GIC fund as a bond substitute.

CHAPTER 10

Ninety Percent of the Ball Game

Professional athletes and coaches are fond of pointing out that what really matters in their specialty isn't always what the fans think. Watch enough basketball and you're likely to hear that the game is 90% defense (or free-throw-shooting or passing or some other pedestrian part of the game). Football fans are apt to hear that 90% of football games are decided by the linemen or special teams. And every baseball fan knows the classic insight attributed to former New York Yankee Yogi Berra: "Ninety percent of baseball is mental. The other half is physical."

Investment pros also like to parse their game into its constituent parts. But being numbers people, they tend to be more precise about it. In fact, in a celebrated 1991 study of the returns earned by pension fund managers, researchers statistically *proved* what 90% of investing is. It is asset allocation.

Asset allocation refers to the way you divide your money among the stock funds, bond funds, and capital preservation funds in your 401(k). The researchers found that the investment mix accounted for 91.5% of the variation in total return among the pension plans they surveyed. Security selection (whether the pension managers chose stocks or bonds that did better or worse than the pack) and market timing (when they decided to buy and sell stocks or bonds) together explained a measly 6.2% of the managers' returns.

As often happens in the world of academic finance, the study has triggered a fierce debate hinging on fine points of statistics. In this case, the issue is whether the 91.5% figure is precisely correct. We can't settle the debate here, and in the end it doesn't matter. Whether the number really ought to be 91.5% or 76.5% or something less, no one disputes the central thesis of the study is indisputable: Asset allocation plays a major role in determining your investment results, especially in a 401(k).

Why the Mix Matters Most

That conclusion may at first sound as improbable as attributing the San Francisco 49ers' success to their cheerleaders. After all, had you bought Intel stock, say, in the spring of 1994, you'd have more than doubled your money over the next 14 months. Had you bought stock in the retailer Bradlees instead, you'd have lost 90%. How, you may wonder, could that *not* be more important than asset allocation?

The problem with such observations is that people always make them in retrospect. If you look back in time, *of course* you will find stocks or mutual funds that blew the doors off the competition. And *of course* there will be moments when it would have paid off tremendously to switch your money from one type of asset to another. The real question is, is there any sign that anyone can consistently make those brilliant calls in advance? Obviously not, as any honest investment manager will tell you. The most successful mutual fund under continuous management since 1980 earned an average of 21.8% a year as of late-1996—which suggests that even the brainiest managers have a hard time keeping their portfolios brimming with Intels or jumping on cue from one winning asset category to the next. (Nevertheless, many investors can't resist the temptation to try timing the market; the tutorial below explains why all such efforts eventually fail.)

Why Market Timing Doesn't Work

One of the most persistent and seductive fallacies of investing is market timing: the notion that you can improve your returns by putting your money into stock funds when the market is going up and shifting into something safer when the market is headed down. Granted, *if* you could do it consistently, you'd be rich beyond your dreams. But you can't.

Why not? After all, you have to choose between only two investment choices, stocks and capital preservation funds, at the beginning of each year. Why has no one been able to make money for an extended period by doing that? There are several reasons:

- Harkening back to investing Principle No. 5 in Chapter 5, it's impossible to forecast short-term changes in the markets. As a result, it's unrealistic to expect a market timer to choose correctly between stocks and capital preservation funds more than 50% of the time in the long run.
- However, because the stock market rises in two out of three years, you have to be right much more often than half the time to keep up with a strategy of simply buying stock funds and holding on.
- But it's actually even tougher than that. An astonishingly large proportion of the stock market's gains occur in very brief spurts. A buy-and-hold investor in the 1980s would have enjoyed average annual gains of 17.6%. If that investor had missed just the 10 biggest days in that entire decade, the return would have sunk to 12.5% a year. If you missed the 20 biggest days, your return would have shriveled to 9.4%.
- To make things even more difficult, most of the big daily moves occur right at the very beginning of a rally, a moment when most market timers are still playing it safe.

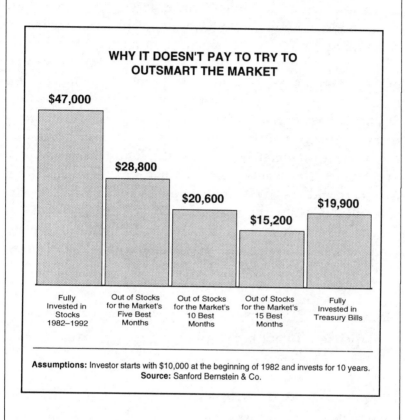

WHY IT DOESN'T PAY TO TRY TO OUTSMART THE MARKET

$47,000	$28,800	$20,600	$15,200	$19,900
Fully Invested in Stocks 1982–1992	Out of Stocks for the Market's Five Best Months	Out of Stocks for the Market's 10 Best Months	Out of Stocks for the Market's 15 Best Months	Fully Invested in Treasury Bills

Assumptions: Investor starts with $10,000 at the beginning of 1982 and invests for 10 years.
Source: Sanford Bernstein & Co.

One of the allures of market timing is that it supposedly will spare you the pain of periodic market downturns. But in fact, it's much more important to capture all of the market's gains than to miss the occasional downturn. Investing is one sport where the players on the sidelines are the ones most likely to get hurt.

Once you rule out psychic powers among money managers, the central importance of asset allocation starts to make more sense. In the long run, portfolios of stocks will behave more like one another than like portfolios of bonds—and vice versa. So in most cases the long-term difference in return among stock funds in your 401(k) will be insignificant compared to the long-term difference between your stock funds and your bond funds. The obvious conclusion: What matters most in your 401(k)'s ultimate growth is how you split your money among stocks, bonds, and capital preservation funds—and not which funds of each type you choose.

This suggests that a lot of people approach the investments in their 401(k) the wrong way. It is still certainly important to understand the specific funds that your plan offers you. You want to know what return and risk level to expect and to have some grasp of why they behave the way they do. But the first decision you have to make is how to apportion your money among the funds in the plan. And the way to do that isn't to examine your 401(k)'s funds; it is to examine yourself.

Taking Your Own Measure as an Investor

If short-term risk pays off with long-term return, the way to maximize your returns should be to take maximum risks. So why shouldn't you just press your 401(k)'s pedal to the floor and put all your money into the most aggressive stock fund? You could, and odds are that you could get a higher return than you would with any other allocation of your 401(k)—if you could hold on long enough.

But that may be a bigger "if" than you thought. Many top aggressive growth funds plunged 30% or more in one month during the market crash of 1987; the average equity fund lost 21%. Not every investor could stand to see his or her retirement fund suddenly laid waste like that. How you would bear up under that kind of loss—your **risk**

tolerance, in financial-planning jargon—is the first judgment call you have to make in setting your 401(k)'s asset mix.

While a small industry of financial planners, benefits specialists, and others all peddle quizzes and software programs designed to help investors evaluate their risk tolerance, the issue boils down to three questions:

1. *How soon do you need to get at your money?* The longer you plan to keep your money invested, the more you can afford to put at risk in your plan's stock funds. With a lead of five years or more, the stock market has time to recover from most of the interim pratfalls it may take. In addition, the longer your time frame, the more likely you are to be rewarded for taking the risks of stock market investing.

2. *What's the likelihood that you'll need the money sooner than you think?* Nothing can wreck your investing experience as surely as being forced by an unexpected expense to withdraw money from your stock funds at the bottom of a sour market.

That's why, when you assess your tolerance for risk, you should also take a look at your overall financial circumstances. Is your job secure? Could you call on resources other than your 401(k) to see you through a cash squeeze? (As Chapter 11 explains, pulling money out of your 401(k) can be extremely expensive, even if you're not forced to sell into a crashing market.) If the answers are no, you should take less risk in your 401(k) than your time frame alone might indicate. Conversely, if your industry is growing and demand for your job skills is high, you can feel more confident that you can ride out any downturn in the stock market.

Chapter 4 mentions some inexpensive steps you can take to bolster your financial security before you put even a penny into your plan. One of the most basic is to squirrel away three to six months' living expenses in a safe, readily accessible investment outside your 401(k), like a money-market fund or U.S. savings bond. This cash reserve should be enough to tide you and your family over if you are laid up or laid off. You should also make sure that you have adequate insurance: health care coverage, homeowners or renters insurance, and—equally important but often over-looked—a disability policy that will replace 60% or so of your salary if you are disabled and can't do your job for an extended period.

3. *How much money could you lose before losing your cool?* If retirement is still a decade or more in the future and you are reasonably secure in your job, you should have no trouble shrugging off a one-year loss of 10% or 20% on a stock fund. You know that you have plenty of time to make up the loss. At least that's the theory.

But when a real live market crash starts to vaporize your money, theory often goes out the window. Emotion takes over. At some point you stop thinking about the long-term performance of stocks and how stocks have always bounced back from previous downturns. You start to focus on one thing: getting out with the rest of your nest egg intact.

That's why it's crucial that you be realistic about your psychological threshold of pain. Could you tough out a market like 1973–1974 without selling out of your stock funds? Are you willing to wake up one New Year's Day and realize that your 401(k) account is 25% smaller than it was the previous year? Or would you reach your emotional limit at 20%, 15%, or 10%?

Once you've answered that question, you have to con-struct a 401(k) account that isn't likely to send you over the red line, even if the stock market plunges. Remember, the biggest threat to your 401(k)'s long-range return isn't that your stock funds will lose money over a decade or more.

(It could happen, but it's unlikely.) The more serious risk is that you'll succumb to the all-too-human temptation to flee a losing market, and you'll miss the rebound. You'll end up capturing all the short-term risk of the stock market while missing out on much of the growth potential. As Peter Lynch, former manager of Fidelity's Magellan mutual fund and one of the greatest investors of his generation, puts it: "The key to making money in stocks is not to be scared out of them."

The Alchemy of Diversification

So, one answer to the question of why it might not be wise just to pour all your money into your plan's most aggressive stock funds is that you might not be able to handle the risk, and you'll do the wrong thing at just the wrong time. But there's an even better reason not to try it: You don't have to. The first law of investing—namely, that reward is commensurate with risk—has a loophole. It's called the **diversification effect**, and it says that you can get nearly as strong a return with far less risk by spreading your money around among the investment options of your plan.

The diversification effect works because a portfolio is more than just the sum of its parts. No two funds in your 401(k) react identically to the same economic or market stimulus. (At least that's the case if your employer has done a good job selecting funds for your plan.) As a result, gains in one fund can often offset losses in another, and the two combined produce a more appealing trade-off between risk and reward than either fund alone.

An example: According to the Chicago investment research firm Ibbotson Associates, between 1972 and 1994 long-term Treasury bonds returned an annualized 8.6%, with a standard deviation of 11.9. (A reminder: Standard deviation measures risk by recording the assets' range of returns over a given period. A standard deviation of 11.9 means that most of the bonds' annual returns fell within 11.9 percentage points of their average annual return, or between −3% and a little over 20%.) By comparison, a portfolio that was composed of roughly two-thirds large-company stocks with the remainder split between Treasury bonds and Treasury bills would have had exactly the same standard deviation as the bond-only portfolio—but would have returned nearly two percentage points a year more.

To make diversification work, you don't necessarily need a wide variety of different funds in your 401(k). You do, however, need funds that behave differently from one another—funds whose returns have relatively low *correlation* with each other, as statisticians would say. The measurement of correlation—or how much different investments move in lockstep with one another—ranges from 1.0 for assets that mirror each other's moves perfectly to −1.0 for those that perform exactly opposite from one another. As a result, a portfolio consisting of a small-company stock fund and a large-company fund would not be particularly diversified, since the two assets are highly correlated with each other (0.77). But adding Treasury bills to the portfolio would pack a powerful diversification effect because bills have a slightly negative correlation with both kinds of stock funds.

One unexpected benefit of diversification is that adding a relatively risky fund can actually lower a portfolio's risk as well as increase its expected return. If you add a small contingent of stocks to a portfolio that is 100% bonds, for example, you wind up with a less risky portfolio—and one that you would expect to have a higher return. The effect is especially striking when you add international stocks to

CORRELATIONS OF MAJOR ASSET CLASSES

	Large-Company Stocks	Small-Company Stocks	International Stocks	Intermediate-Term Bonds	Treasury Bills
Large-company stocks	1.00				
Small-company stocks	.77	1.00			
International stocks	.56	.41	1.00		
Intermediate-term bonds	.48	.23	.12	1.00	
Treasury bills	.02	−.10	−.18	.32	1.0

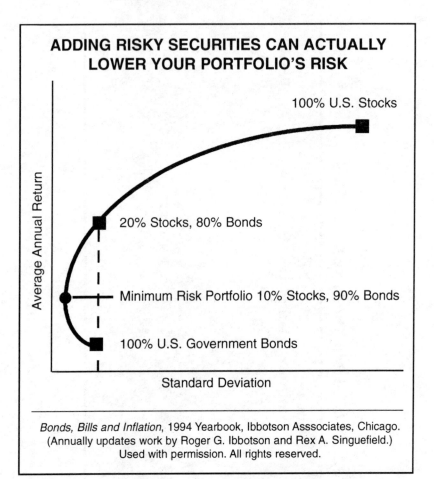

ADDING RISKY SECURITIES CAN ACTUALLY LOWER YOUR PORTFOLIO'S RISK

100% U.S. Stocks

20% Stocks, 80% Bonds

Minimum Risk Portfolio 10% Stocks, 90% Bonds

100% U.S. Government Bonds

Average Annual Return

Standard Deviation

Bonds, Bills and Inflation, 1994 Yearbook, Ibbotson Asssociates, Chicago. (Annually updates work by Roger G. Ibbotson and Rex A. Singuefield.) Used with permission. All rights reserved.

a 401(k) account made up entirely of domestic funds. Even though by themselves international stock funds are among the riskiest types of funds in 401(k)s, their correlation with U.S. securities is so low (0.53) that they have a powerful diversifying effect—often simultaneously lowering your account's risk and raising its expected return.

Matching Your Money and Your Moxie

Your goal in choosing an asset allocation is to come up with a mix that gives you the highest return you can get at a risk level you can stand. Unfortunately, like much else in investing, constructing such a portfolio is more art than science.

Not that it can't be made to look scientific. Armed with a computer and data on returns, volatility, and correlations among types of investments, financial planners can calculate the expected returns and risk levels of a virtually infinite number of portfolios and then select the one that promises to deliver the return you desire at the lowest level of risk. In fact, the portfolios in this chapter were generated by the financial-planning firm of Bingham, Osborn & Scarborough in San Francisco using similar software and historical performance records. Some large 401(k) plans make simplified versions of the software available to their employees.

A caution: Don't be misled by the apparent precision of the portfolios these programs generate. Their expected returns and risk levels are not promises. They are projections based on the past, and in the investment business the past gives you at best a very general idea of what to expect. In short, regard the portfolios in this book—or, for that matter, others that you encounter in off-the-shelf software or in your plan's educational materials—merely as suggestions, not templates for your own asset allocations.

The following portfolios span three levels of risk, corresponding to different phases in a typical lifetime of saving and spending. Since 401(k)s vary widely in the number and type of investment options, the portfolios at each phase come in two versions: the generic model, which includes just T-bills, bonds, and stocks, and the five-fund model, which includes funds typically found only in plans with a broad selection. Even so, you may have to do considerable shimming and trimming to fit the models into the real choices offered in your plan. (The table on page 153 should help you make some translations.) And, of course, you must be the judge of how these three portfolios address your own financial situation and tolerance of risk. In the end, however, the future of your 401(k) account is likely to ride on asset mixes that look something like these.

THE GO-FOR-IT PORTFOLIO: MORE THAN 10 YEARS FROM WITHDRAWAL

This phase of your 401(k) buildup can last from your first contribution until you reach your mid–fifties—or even later if you plan to keep the money invested until you are well into retirement. Your motto should be maximum inflation-beating return at a risk level that allows you to stay on course. Accordingly, the portfolio is tilted overwhelmingly toward stock funds. The five–fund portfolio, for example, has 75% of its assets in three types of stock funds; the generic has 75% in its lone stock entry.

Risk is part of the game at this phase. The five-fund allocation would have cost you money in four of the 25 calendar years included in the data. The worst was a 16% flop in 1974, and in 1973 and 1974 combined you would have lost 28%. Even so, the risk-dampening effects of diversification are clear. For example, the portfolio's losses are far less severe than those of, say, small-company stocks alone, which dove 45% in 1973 and 1974. But the portfolio's return trails that of the small-company index by only a percentage point a year on average.

Note the diversification effect at work in the results of the generic portfolio and the five-fund version. The only basic difference between the two is that the five-slice pie

HOW TO MATCH YOUR INVESTMENT OPTIONS TO THE SUGGESTED PORTFOLIOS

If the suggested portfolio calls for this kind of fund . . .	. . . your 401(k)'s closest choice may be called this
Large-company stock	Blue-chip fund Growth fund Equity-index fund Core equity fund	Equity fund Growth and income fund Equity-income fund Balanced fund (stock portion)
Small-company stock	Aggressive growth Small-cap fund	Maximum growth Maximum capital-gains fund
International stock Intermediate–bond fund	Global equity Intermediate-term bond U.S. government bond★ Corporate bond★ Balanced fund (bond portion) Stable-value or GIC fund (if no bond fund is offered)	World stock Bond index Income fund Bond fund★
Capital preservation or cash	Stable-value or GIC fund (if a bond fund is available) Money-market fund Cash reserves fund	

★In a 401(k), these will usually be intermediate-term funds, but double-check with your benefits administrator for your particular plan. Longer-maturity funds will be riskier than intermediate-term alternatives.

THE GO-FOR-IT PORTFOLIO

(More than 10 years from withdrawal)

FIVE-FUND PORTFOLIO

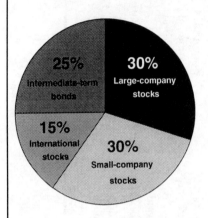

Annualized total return (1970–94): 12.2%
Margin over inflation: 6.5%
Normal range of annual returns: −1.3% to 25.7%
Worst single year (1974): −16.0%
Best single year (1975): 34.7%
Bear market (1973–74): −28.4%

GENERIC PORTFOLIO

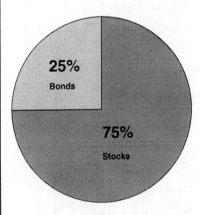

Annualized total return (1970–94): 10.7%
Margin over inflation: 5.0%
Normal range of annual returns: −1.8% to 23.2%
Worst single year (1974): −18.6%
Best single year (1975): 30.0%
Bear market (1973–74): −26.7%

Assumptions: Portfolio is reset to desired ratios at the beginning of each year.
Sources: Bingham, Osborn & Scarborough, San Francisco; Ibbotson & Associates, SBBI 1994 Yearbook; Chase Investment Performance Digest, 1994.

includes two ultrarisky equity categories, small-company stock funds and internationals. But because of their imperfect correlation with each other and the rest of the portfolio, the two additional funds would have given the portfolio a significantly higher return for only a modest increase in risk.

THE CRUISING SPEED PORTFOLIO: 10 YEARS FROM WITHDRAWAL

As you begin to draw within 10 years of needing the money, you have to take into account your diminished ability to recover from a sharp market blow. You want your 401(k) to continue growing faster than inflation, so stocks should remain your dominant investment. However, you can't afford to stick your neck out quite so far as before.

The five-fund portfolio plays it safer by dropping the percentage committed to stocks from 75% to 60% and sharply cutting the portion of the equity stake committed to small stocks from 30% to 20%. The generic portfolio pulls in its equity horns by a similar amount. In both portfolios the changes reduce volatility by about 15–20%, down to roughly the level of long-term bonds. But diversification continues to work its magic: the portfolios' returns (again, based on their historical track record) were more than 1½ to 2 percentage points a year higher than that of the bonds.

The key to making the transition from the earlier portfolio to this one is to do it in stages spread over a year or 18 months. If your plan permits you to change your assets quarterly or more often, map out how you want your money divided at each stage and then shift enough money from your stock funds to the bond fund to match those interim allocations. (See the table on page 157 for an example of how you might do this.) If your plan permits changes

155

THE CRUISING SPEED PORTFOLIO

(10 years from withdrawal)

FIVE-FUND PORTFOLIO

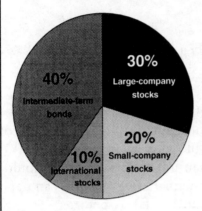

30%
Large-company stocks

40%
Intermediate-term bonds

10%
International stocks

20%
Small-company stocks

Annualized total return (1970–94): 11.5%
Margin over inflation: 5.8%
Normal range of annual returns: 0.4% to 22.6%
Worst single year (1974): –12.2%
Best single year (1975): 29.3%
Bear market (1973–74): –21.1%

GENERIC PORTFOLIO

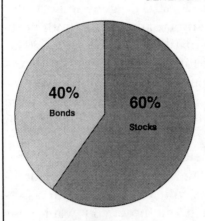

40%
Bonds

60%
Stocks

Annualized total return (1970–94): 10.5%
Margin over inflation: 4.8%
Normal range of annual returns: –0.3% to 21.3%
Worst single year (1974): –14.0%
Best single year (1985): 27.8%
Bear market (1973–74): –20.1%

Assumptions: Portfolio is reset to desired ratios at the beginning of each year.
Sources: Bingham, Osborn & Scarborough, San Francisco; Ibbotson & Associates, SBBI 1994 Yearbook; Chase Investment Performance Digest, 1994.

MOVE GRADUALLY WHEN REALIGNING YOUR PORTFOLIO

	Starting Allocation	Transition after . . .			New Allocation
		Three Months	Six Months	Nine Months	
Large-co. stocks	30	30	30	30	30
Small-co. stocks	30	27.5	25	22.5	20
Foreign stocks	15	12.5	10	10	10
Int. term bonds	25	30	35	37.5	40

only annually, then make the shift in two stages. By spreading out the transition, you eliminate the risk of bad timing—that you could happen to transfer 15% of your portfolio out of stocks, say, just before a bull market.

THE HOLD-THE-LINE PORTFOLIO: ONCE WITHDRAWALS START

Once you start to rely on your retirement savings for living expenses, safety becomes paramount—but safety in the broadest investment sense. You have to protect your nest egg from short-term market risk, to be sure. But you also need your money to last as long as you do—perhaps another 25 years if you retire at age 65. That means you need to maintain inflation-beating returns on the balance of your portfolio even as you begin to draw money out. (You'll find more on the proper approach to investing in retirement in Chapter 12.)

As a result, stocks remain a sizable presence in the portfolio. Over the past 25 years, the 30% stake envisioned here would have kept the portfolio at least four percentage points a year ahead of inflation, on average. At that rate of return, your money would hold up for 27 years, assuming 4%

THE HOLD-YOUR-OWN PORTFOLIO

(As withdrawals begin)

FIVE-FUND PORTFOLIO

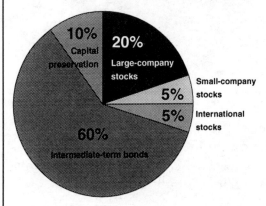

Annualized total return
(1970–94): 10.1%
Margin over inflation: 4.4%
Normal range of annual
returns: 2.7% to 17.5%
Worst single year (1974): –3.6%
Best single year (1985): 24.8%
Bear market (1973–74): –5.6%

GENERIC PORTFOLIO

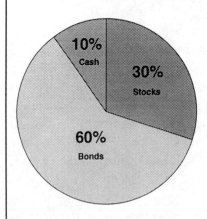

Annualized total return (1970–94): 9.7%
Margin over inflation: 4.0%
Normal range of expected annual
returns: 2.1% to 17.3%
Worst single year (1974): –4.2%
Best single year (1982): 17.3%
Bear market (1973–74): –5.3%

Assumptions: Portfolio is reset to desired ratios at the beginning of each year.
Sources: Bingham, Osborn & Scarborough, San Francisco; Ibbotson &
Associates, SBBI 1994 Yearbook; Chase Investment Performance Digest, 1994.

inflation and that you withdraw 6% of your money the first year and increase your withdrawals by the rate of inflation each year thereafter. Market risk would have been reduced markedly, though it wouldn't have vanished: in the bear market of 1973 and 1974, the portfolio would have dipped 5.6%.

As you move deeper into retirement and your need to keep a long-term edge on inflation fades, you can move even more of your assets into intermediate-term bonds and capital preservation funds. But stocks can never vanish from your portfolio—and as a result, neither can all market risk. In a world in which inflation remains ineradicable, some market risk is the price you pay to maintain the value of your money.

Off-the-Rack Asset Allocations

To help employees who don't feel comfortable tailoring their own portfolios, many money managers now include so-called life cycle funds among the wares they present to employers sponsoring 401(k) plans. These consist of three or more funds, typically representing an aggressive, moderate, or conservative asset allocation. The T. Rowe Price Personal Strategy Funds, for example, consist of portfolios roughly comparable to the three suggested in this chapter: a growth fund (80% stocks, 20% bonds), a balanced fund (60% stocks, 30% bonds, and 10% money-market), and an income fund (40% stocks, 40% bonds, and 20% money-market). Each fund can vary as much as 10% in either direction from those settings, depending on the fund manager's outlook. In every life cycle fund, you're encouraged to move from the most aggressive to the least aggressive portfolio as you draw closer to needing the money.

About 2% of plans offer life cycle funds, and more sponsors are planning to introduce them. If you are really paralyzed at the thought of choosing your own asset allocation, they can help. But be careful: The funds designed for people your age may not be a perfect fit for you. You should make your own decisions, based on the more relevant issues of how soon you need the money or how psychologically equipped you are to handle the risk level assigned to people your age.

The 10-Minute Portfolio Manager

Once you've chosen an asset allocation, don't do much tinkering with it. Above all, resist the urge to widen or narrow the slices of your pie in response to developments in the market. The temptation will always be to make the wrong call at the wrong time—to commit less of your money to stock funds *after* a market sell-off, for example. Such **tactical asset allocation**, as it's known, amounts to market timing in disguise. Disguised or not, it's hard to pull off successfully for more than a few tries.

On the other hand, your portfolio *will* require periodic checkups and maintenance. That's because the ups and downs of your various funds will eventually cause your asset allocation to drift away from what you originally intended. For example, if you started 1991 with 75% of your money in stocks and 25% in bonds, by late 1995 the differing movements in those two markets would have shifted you to 80% stocks and 20% bonds. Without really noticing, you gradually acquired a riskier portfolio.

REBALANCING YOUR PORTFOLIO

	Intended Allocation	Initial Amount	Return	Year-end Investment	Year-end Allocation	Needed Change
Large-co. stocks	30%	$30,000	10%	$33,000	29.6%	+ $450
Small-co. stocks	30%	$30,000	25%	$37,500	33.6%	− $4,050
Foreign stocks	15%	$15,000	− 5%	$14,250	12.8%	+ $2,475
Int. term bonds	25%	$25,000	7%	$26,750	24.0%	+ $1,125

The solution: Compare your actual asset allocation with your original plan at least once a year. If you find that the percentages have changed, shift around enough money to make the funds line up again. This is called **rebalancing** your portfolio, and it serves two useful purposes. First, it keeps you from gradually taking on more investment risk than you intended. Over time your riskier funds will tend to have higher returns, and if left unattended, they'll come to dominate your portfolio.

Second, by its nature rebalancing means that you sell the funds that have had the biggest run and reinvest in those that have done relatively poorly. That's a way of forcing you to do what every investor sets out to do: Buy low and sell high. Indeed, one recent study showed that rebalancing your portfolio would add between one-quarter and nearly one-half a percentage point a year to your total return.

How Your 401(k) Fits In

While your 401(k) is probably your best retirement investment, it shouldn't be your only one. Over time you may also acquire other mutual funds, stocks, savings bonds, and so on. The efficient way to manage your entire lineup of long-term investments is to think of them as constituting one megaportfolio, of which your 401(k) is just one part.

This sounds more complicated than it really is. It basically means that you should be conscious of your 401(k) assets when you make outside investments, and vice versa. So if your 401(k) does not offer an international stock fund, for example, it makes sense to fill that gap by earmarking some of your outside investment dollars to internationals. Similarly, if your 401(k) is freighted with your employer's stock—which can happen if your company makes its matching contributions only in the form of company stock—you should avoid buying any shares of the stock with your outside money. In fact, it's probably wise to avoid all stocks in the same industry as your company.

One often repeated but misguided piece of advice is that you should keep your interest-bearing investments such as bonds and capital preservation funds inside the tax shelter of your 401(k) and do your equity investing in your outside portfolio.

The advice seems logical at first, because the tax code treats interest or dividend income more harshly than it treats capital gains. Interest and dividends become part of your taxable income the year you receive them and are subject to your maximum tax bracket, which could be as high as 39.6%. By contrast, you don't have to add capital gains to your income tax return until you *realize* them—that is, cash them out—and even then your tax rate tops out at a special capital-gains tax rate, of 28%.

162

In other words, it's possible to defer paying taxes on appreciation in your stock funds whether you hold them inside a 401(k) or not, while the only way to get tax deferral on an income fund is to invest in it under the shelter of your 401(k). As a result, the common wisdom holds that you make best use of your 401(k)'s tax advantages if you concentrate your income-oriented investments inside your plan.

A warning, though: The common wisdom works only if you are a strict buy-and-hold investor outside your 401(k). If you tend to sell your stocks in less than three years or so (as most investors do), then you will continually be recognizing capital gains—and being taxed on them, if you own the stocks outside your 401(k) or IRAs. So unless you rarely cash in your profits on your non-401(k) investments, forget about trying to gain a tax edge by leaning toward income investments in your 401(k). Instead, invest your 401(k) for maximum returns and let the taxes fall where and when they might.

KEY POINTS

- The most important investment decision you make in managing your 401(k) is the asset-allocation decision: how you will divide your money among your plan's various investment options.
- Keep in mind the importance of diversification. You can reduce your risk and often increase your return if you spread your money among funds that tend to respond differently to the same stimulus. That way, gains in one fund will offset losses in another.
- Keep the bulk of your investments in the stock market when you are more than 10 years from needing the money in your plan. Gradually shift to a more conserva-

tive mix of investments as you get closer to withdrawing the money.
- Periodically check your 401(k)'s asset allocation, pruning back funds that have grown beyond their intended allocation and adding money to those that have fallen behind.

CHAPTER 11

How to Get Your Money Back

You would not be reading this book if you hadn't already decided that a sound retirement was a serious goal. You've probably also signed on to the idea that you need to start saving for it now, even if retirement won't begin for another few decades. But, still. The idea of locking your money away all those years can make even a dedicated saver feel queasy. What if you have triplets and need a bigger house? What if you get sick? What if your daughter gets accepted at Harvard without a scholarship? Would you be able to get at your money?

Yes, you would—but on terms set by Uncle Sam and your company, not you. To justify handing out tax breaks to 401(k) participants, the government wants the savings used mainly to fund retirement. To discourage their use for other purposes, the tax code has installed some formidable safeguards. The general rule is, as long as you are working for a plan's sponsor, you can't get at your tax-deferred contributions or the earnings on that money except in very specific circumstances. When you do, you could very well owe taxes on every penny you withdraw, and if you are under age 59½ at the time, you also have to come up with a 10% tax penalty.

This being the U.S. tax code, however, there are multiple loopholes and exceptions. If you need the money to pay for unreimbursed medical bills that exceed 7½% of your income or if you are severely disabled, you can take your money out without the 10% penalty. Likewise, your beneficiaries escape the penalty if you die and leave them the money (although this is a pretty drastic step to take just to avoid taxes). If you divorce and your 401(k) assets are divided up in the settlement, your ex-spouse is allowed to withdraw his or her allotment without penalty. You can also dodge the 10% haircut if you are 55 or older and leave your job.

One other loophole works at any age, but it's rarely used. If you take your money out of the plan in substantially equal payments designed to last the rest of your expected life span, Uncle Sam waives the tax penalty. Assuming your company permits this kind of withdrawal, you (and your tax adviser) need to consult IRS life expectancy tables to find out how much you have to take out each year. But don't get too excited. The money available to you in any given year won't be very much unless you start pulling it out in your fifties anyway, and once you start making these lifelong withdrawals, you must keep them up at their steady pace for at least five years or until you reach age 59½, whichever is later. If you don't, the IRS will regard everything you withdrew as an early distribution, and you'll be back in the penalty box.

As you can see, the loopholes in the tax code apply only in very specific circumstances. Fortunately, most plans have optional provisions that let you withdraw meaningful chunks of unpenalized money without having to die or divorce or retire first. If your plan permits after-tax contributions, for example, it probably also lets you take the money out with little fuss, since you didn't receive any tax break for making the contributions in the first place. The rules are stickier for pretax contributions. Even so, nearly nine out of 10 plans permit so-called hardship withdrawals, and three out of four offer what is probably the most appealing temporary escape hatch, a 401(k) loan.

A word of caution: All of these options have drawbacks, the *least* serious of which is that they can set back the growth of your 401(k) by years. Remember, your 401(k) is the foundation of the savings edifice that will help shelter you and keep you fed once your salary stops. Don't chip away at it without a very good reason.

Withdrawals of After-Tax Savings

While the number of plans that permit after-tax contributions is dwindling, those that still allow them generally let you take that money out for any reason. If you do make a withdrawal, you won't owe taxes on the contributions themselves, since you already paid taxes on them. Even so, withdrawals of after-tax money are not entirely bloodless, taxwise. Depending on how your plan accounts for withdrawals and whether you made any after-tax contributions before 1987 (believe me, you don't want the explanation), you may have to count a surprisingly large piece of your withdrawal as taxable income. In one of the simpler scenarios, for example, an after-tax withdrawal would be taxed as if it consisted of after-tax contributions, investment earnings, and pretax contributions in the same proportions in which they exist in your plan. Both pretax contributions and investment earnings are subject to full taxes and the 10% tax penalty.

Moral: Don't make after-tax contributions to your 401(k)

intending to pull your money out within a few years. Because you'll have to pay taxes and penalties on a portion of the withdrawal from your after-tax account, you are usually better off saving for near-term expenses in regular taxable investments—unless your company matches your after-tax contributions. If you have your eye on an expense that's seven years away or farther, you're better off making pretax contributions and claiming the extra tax boost they confer. You could then meet the expense out of pretax money by making a hardship withdrawal or taking out a loan.

Hardship Withdrawals

Employers may let you take pretax money out of your account while you're still working to respond to an "immediate and heavy" financial need. Though each company can set its own rules for what constitutes acceptably grave need, most plans simply abide by federal guidelines. The four expenses that Uncle Sam automatically approves are

- to pay college tuition for yourself or a dependent
- to purchase your primary residence
- to cover unreimbursed medical expenses
- to prevent foreclosure on or eviction from your primary residence.

The hardship exceptions seem sensibly humanitarian, but they come with lots of strings attached. For starters, you won't qualify for them unless you're so hard up that you can't get the money from any other source, including any 401(k) loans. The IRS leaves it up to your employer to verify this. Depending on the rules of the plan, the company can either require you to document both the expense and the fact that you don't have any money to cover it, or it can simply suspend you from making contributions to the plan for a full year (under the presumption, apparently, that you'd never agree to such a self-destructive thing unless you were really desperate).

As for taxes, hardship cases get no special mercy from the IRS. You'll have to pay income taxes in the year you pull out the money, and you may face the dread 10% penalty. Keep that in mind when you figure out how much you need to withdraw. The company will withhold 20% of your money for taxes, but that could just be the down payment for the bill you'll get next April 15. For example, if you are in the 33% tax bracket (counting federal, state, and local taxes) you would have to withdraw more than $32,000 to lay your hands on $20,000. The rest of the money would be needed to cover the 20% withholding, the income taxes in excess of the withholding, and the tax penalty. Such withdrawals may be a hardship for you, but they're a windfall for the IRS.

Loans

A loan, if your company permits, is a far less traumatic way to take money out of your plan. You typically can borrow as much as $50,000 or half the money in your account. The term is five years, unless you are borrowing to buy your principal residence. In that case you may have as long as 10 to 30 years to pay off the loan.

In contrast with a hardship withdrawal, a loan may be approved for any reason, and you don't have to pay any taxes on the money you receive as long as you pay it back. The interest rate is reasonable, too—typically, one or two percentage points above the benchmark rate for bank loans known as the **prime rate**, compared with six points or more above prime for an unsecured personal loan at a bank.

Best of all, the interest you pay typically goes right back into your account, not into the coffers of some bank. It's as if a portion of your 401(k) were partly invested in a GIC issued by you. (In a few plans, the interest you pay is instead credited to a special fund made up of all outstanding participant loans pooled together; each 401(k) borrower is credited with a proportionate share of the total interest earned by the pool.)

But hold a minute before you dial up your benefits administrator. Loans have some serious drawbacks. For starters, the loan can turn extremely expensive if you don't pay it back on time. There's not much risk you'll default while you're still working for the company because the payments are usually deducted automatically from your paycheck. But if you leave your job, even if you leave at your company's invitation—that is, if you are laid off or fired—you will have to pay off the balance promptly in full. Otherwise the IRS will treat the outstanding balance as a withdrawal, subject to all the usual taxes and penalties.

Another potentially high cost comes in a less obvious form: the investment growth that you may forgo because of the loan—what economists refer to as **opportunity cost**. Could the burden of paying back your loan cause you to stop contributing to your plan? If so, that's one way a loan may undercut the long-term buildup of your 401(k).

That will also happen if your account as a whole grows at a rate exceeding the interest you pay on the loan. While it's not possible for you to know in advance, a loan to yourself at one percentage point over prime may not be as profitable as an investment in your 401(k)'s stock and bond funds. If it's not, you will retire with a smaller nest egg than if you had left your account alone. That's a potential cost many 401(k) borrowers don't take into account.

In the real world, however, you do sometimes need seri-

HOW TO GET YOUR MONEY OUT BEFORE RETIREMENT

Type of Withdrawal	10% Early Withdrawal Penalty?	Ordinary Income Taxes?	Must Employer Allow?	Drawbacks
Distribution at death	No	Yes	Yes	Not bad for your heirs: extremely inconvenient for you.
Distribution upon diagnosis of disability	No	Yes	Yes	The disability must be permanent and severe.
Distribution for medical emergency	No	Yes	Yes	Must be for deductible medical expenses that exceed 7.5% of your adjusted gross income.
Equal withdrawals spread over your expected life span	No	Yes	No	The yearly amount you can access is likely to be tiny unless you are already close to age 59½.
Hardship withdrawals	Yes	Yes	No	For limited purposes only. Plus you may have to prove hardship or suspend contributions for a year.
Loan	No	No	No	You must repay the loan with interest, typically over five years.
Withdrawal upon leaving your job before retirement	Yes	Yes	No	Monster tax bill to pay; consider only in emergencies.
Rollover to new employer's 401(k) upon leaving your job	No	No	No	Your new employer may not accept the rollover until you qualify for its plan, which may not be for a year.
Rollover to IRA upon leaving your job	No	No	No	Unless you have the money sent directly to your IRA trustee, your company will withhold 20% for taxes.

ous sums of money in a short time, and a 401(k) loan is more efficient than many of your other options. But before you even consider borrowing against your account, make sure that you can afford to keep up both the loan payments and your regular contributions. Also make sure that you have enough money available from outside sources to pay off the loan immediately if you were to change jobs or—God forbid—be laid off.

Also, if you have considerable equity in your home and a relatively clean credit record, check whether it's cheaper to take out a home-equity loan. The interest rates on these loans, available from just about any bank or mortgage lender, tend to be in the ballpark with 401(k) loans. But you can usually deduct the interest on home-equity loans from your taxes, while you can't do that on 401(k) loans. That can lower the after-tax cost of a home-equity loan considerably.

Here's an example. Suppose you have $50,000 in your 401(k) and can borrow $10,000 against it at 9% over five years. Let's also suppose that you can get exactly the same terms from your bank on a home-equity loan, that you are in the 28% tax bracket, and that the bank loan is tax-deductible. Paying back the 401(k) loan would cost you $2,435 in interest over five years, while it would cost you only $1,768 (after taxes) in the home-equity loan. The home-equity loan saves you enough that even if your 401(k) investments only earn 7% over the next five years—less than you're paying on the 401(k) loan—you will still come out ahead borrowing against your house. (The table on page 175 shows you how home-equity and 401(k) loans stack up at different interest rates.)

Suppose a 401(k) loan nevertheless appears to be your best choice. How do you go about getting one? The process differs from one employer to the next, but it's a lot easier than going to the bank. Some plans will let you apply for the loan over the phone and then send you a check along

COMPARING HOME-EQUITY
AND 401(k) LOANS

If your home-equity loan carries this interest rate . . .	. . . and your 401(k) charges this rate . . .		
	8%	9%	10%
	. . . a home-equity loan works out better as long as your 401(k) balance beats this return		
8%	6%	6.5%	6.5%
9%	7%	7%	7.25%
10%	7.5%	7.75%	8%

Assumptions: Participant takes a $10,000 loan against a $50,000 account, is in the 28% tax bracket, and qualifies to deduct home equity interest.

with some paperwork. Others may require you to fill out an application and perhaps pay a loan origination charge of $10 to $100 and possibly an annual maintenance fee of $15 or so. Many plans limit you to one loan at a time to minimize administrative hassles. If your plan is one of them, make sure you borrow as much as you need. You won't be able to go back to the well more than once.

How quickly you can get the money will depend not only on the loan approval process, but also on how often your plan tots up the values of its various funds. For example, if your plan measures itself at the end of each day, you may be able to get the check within days. If it checks its market value only at the end of each quarter, it may cut checks for borrowers only once every three months. So if you need the money by a specific date, check with your benefits administrator well ahead of time and make sure your schedule tracks with the plan's.

You also want to make sure that borrowing from your

account doesn't throw off your asset allocation—that is, how you've split your money among your plan's investment choices. Some plans let you choose the funds from which the loan will be taken; others automatically deduct the loan amount from one fund, typically one of your income funds. (In the latter case, you may have to transfer enough money from your plan's other funds into that fund before you can take out the loan.) Taking the money out of an income fund makes sense, since a loan to yourself is a kind of debt security. So borrowing from an income fund preserves your asset allocation.

Other companies deduct the loan in equal proportions from all the funds you own. That technique leaves the balance of your 401(k) arrayed in the same proportion as before you borrowed. While that may sound like the least disruptive way of taking money from your account, it actually throws off your asset allocation. Reason: It fails to account for the fact that a more or less significant slice of your account is now invested in a fixed-income asset—namely a loan to yourself. If your plan does things this way, you should compensate by increasing your allocation to equity funds. That will help you keep the same share of your total pie dedicated to the stock market.

What to Do If You Change Jobs

There is one other way you can get at your vested 401(k) money before retirement: You can leave your employer. This is a different circumstance from those we just discussed because it doesn't matter whether or not you need the money; it's usually yours for the taking when you terminate employment. (Companies don't have to let you take your money when you leave before retirement, but most do.)

Fortunately, withdrawal is only one of four options for your 401(k) money at that point. Which one you choose can make a big difference in your financial future.

HAVE THE COMPANY WRITE YOU A CHECK

If your company permits withdrawals at separation of service, as it's called when you leave before retirement, you're entitled to lay your hands on your entire account at this point, though you'd be foolish to do so. Any payout will be subject to full income taxes, plus the 10% penalty. (The only exceptions are the loopholes discussed earlier: if you are 55 or over or are taking your money out of the plan in installments designed to last your lifetime.) All that you accomplish is to chop your retirement money by 25% to 50%, depending on your tax bracket. So unless you desperately need the money, choose one of the other options.

LEAVE THE MONEY WHERE IT IS

Your company has to let you keep your money in its 401(k) plan when you leave work, unless the total of your account comes to less than $5,000. You will continue to get statements and other required documents, just as if you were still employed. However, few employers are thrilled at the prospect of bearing permanent administrative costs for an ex-employee, so in your exit meeting your benefits office may strongly encourage you to take out your money. If that's your company's attitude, you may be better off taking their advice, since you're not likely to be happy with the service you get from benefits officers who wish you would go away. Don't worry, there are other ways to get your money out of the plan without sacrificing a big part of it to the IRS.

TRANSFER THE MONEY INTO YOUR NEW EMPLOYER'S 401(k)

To make this kind of transaction, you first enroll in your new company's plan; then ask the new plan's administrator to arrange for a transfer of your old assets to the new plan. This kind of exchange is known as a **rollover**. (Of course, you can't keep the specific investments you had in the previous plan; you'll have to put your money into the options offered at your new corporate home.) Since you never have access to the money, the IRS does not consider this kind of transfer a taxable distribution. So you're off the hook.

About eight of 10 companies accept rollover contributions. However, some companies may require you to serve a full year before you can sign up for their 401(k). In that case you can either leave your money with your old 401(k) for the year or you can choose the fourth option: You can roll the money over into an Individual Retirement Account. You can then either leave the money in the IRA, where it will grow tax-deferred until retirement, just as it would in your 401(k), or you can roll it over again from your IRA to your new 401(k) when you're eligible for the new plan.

THE IRA ROLLOVER

Moving your 401(k) money directly into an IRA works much the same way as transferring money between 401(k)s. You first set up the account with an IRA trustee—a bank, a mutual fund company, a brokerage, or an independent trustee—and tell them you would like to set up a direct transfer of your 401(k) funds. The IRA trustee and your former company will arrange the rest. You won't lose any of your money to taxes in the process.

If you already have an IRA, make sure to set up a separate IRA for the money you roll over. That's especially important if you are using the IRA as a temporary holding pen while you wait to become eligible for your new company's plan. If you mix the money from a rollover with your own IRA contributions, you close off the option of later rolling the money from your IRA into your new employer's 401(k) or that of some subsequent employer. The reason is that 401(k) contributions may qualify for slightly lighter tax treatment at retirement than IRA savings, and the feds don't want savers converting IRA contributions to 401(k) assets. The IRS isn't in the business of giving away tax breaks.

In theory you could also complete a tax-free rollover by having the company write you a check for the value of your account and then depositing the same amount of money into an IRA within 60 days. But there's one problem: Whenever the company writes you a check for any portion of your 401(k), it has to withhold 20% of the money to cover potential taxes. That's true even if you sincerely plan to roll the money over immediately into an IRA.

What would happen if you got a check and rolled just 80% of your 401(k) balance into an IRA? You would have to come up with the missing 20% elsewhere to deposit in the IRA within the 60-day deadline. Otherwise the IRS would consider the missing 20% a withdrawal and charge you for taxes and perhaps the early withdrawal penalty. So make sure that you have the IRA sponsor and your 401(k) trustee conduct the transfer between themselves.

It's a close call whether it's better to roll over your old 401(k) into an IRA or into your new employer's plan. An IRA gives you an almost unlimited number of investment choices. Open an IRA with a mutual fund family, for example, and you can put your money in any of that family's wares, except municipal bond funds. Choose a brokerage as your trustee, and you have an even wider range of choices, including individual stocks and bonds.

The advantage to rolling into the new 401(k), on the

other hand, is simplicity: You avoid the extra paperwork of having both a 401(k) for your current contributions and an IRA to hold assets from your old employer's plan. If you plan to retire before 2000, you may also pick-up a soon-to-expire but potentially valuable tax break called five- or 10-year averaging. (We'll cover averaging in the next chapter.) It is not available to IRA investors now or to anyone else after 1999.

Ultimately, unless the new 401(k) has unattractive investment options or carries expenses far in excess of what you'd pay for an IRA, you will probably find it simpler and no less profitable to transfer your assets to the new 401(k) plan. Whatever you do with your old 401(k) money when you leave work, however, you should enroll as soon as possible into your new employer's plan. You may be starting a new job, but you can't afford to slack off on the serious work of building a secure future.

KEY POINTS

- Taxes and early withdrawal penalties can make it extremely expensive to take money from your plan while you're still on the job. Do it only as a last resort.
- After-tax contributions are subject to far fewer withdrawal restrictions than pretax contributions. Even so, you still have to pay taxes and possibly a penalty on the earnings your after-tax savings have earned. As a result, it's usually better to save for short-term goals outside your 401(k), unless your employer matches your after-tax contributions.
- Your company may permit you to take money out of the plan for so-called hardship purposes. But even these withdrawals must bear the full brunt of income taxes and early withdrawal penalties.

- A loan is the least damaging way to get at the money in your plan while you're still on the job. But be careful: Taking out a loan may leave you with a smaller 401(k) accumulation than if you had kept the money fully invested.
- You're usually allowed to get at the money when you leave your job, but you shouldn't try. Your best move: Roll the money over into either an IRA or your new employer's 401(k).

CHAPTER 12

Reaping the Rewards

As you draw within five years or so of leaving work, you can start to discern the landscape of the destination called retirement. If you have followed the precepts in this book, that vista should include at least one very pleasing topographical feature: a mountain of cash in your 401(k). Between you and that money, however, lies one more round of difficult decisions. Somehow you have to extract your money from the plan in the manner that best serves your goals and, in the process, puts the most money in your pocket and the least in Uncle Sam's.

Many employees find this endgame to be the toughest and most nerve-racking part of managing a 401(k). At stake is the bulk of your retirement fund—perhaps the single largest pot of money you've ever had. You must negotiate absurdly complicated tax rules, and many of the decisions you face are irreversible: make a mistake and you're stuck with it for the rest of your life. If ever there is any time when it pays to get professional help with your finances, the years before retiring with a fat 401(k) are it. Although this chapter can't take the place of a tax expert's counsel, it can at least alert you to the questions that you will need to answer.

Should You Take Your Money in an Annuity?

Up to this point you have probably thought of your 401(k) as a more or less impressive single sum of money. But the eventual goal of accumulating that pile of money is to convert it into a stream of income that will cover your living expenses in retirement and last as long as you do.

To do this, you have two broad choices. You can pull the money out of your plan in one intact sum, called a **lump-sum distribution**, and take responsibility yourself for mining the lump for income. Virtually every 401(k) plan permits retiring employees to take lump-sum payouts, and in fact, that's what most employees do. (And the majority of them roll the payouts directly over into an IRA.) But some plans offer an alternative, in which the company converts your money into a series of lifelong monthly checks, much like a traditional pension. This is called **annuitizing** your 401(k).

To annuitize, your company will typically purchase an annuity contract from an insurance company with the money in your 401(k). The contract offering the most generous monthly checks is known as a **single-life** annuity. That's basically a check a month for the rest of your life, with the size of the check determined by the sum you are annuitizing, the level of interest rates when you start the annuity, and your life expectancy. However, the law requires employers to give married participants a **joint-and-survivor** annuity, unless the spouse waives his or her right to it in writing. With the joint-and-survivor option, checks arrive as long as *either* you *or* your spouse survive, but the checks typically will be 10% to 15% smaller than from an annuity covering you alone.

Either way, once you or both you and your spouse die, the checks cease. If that prospect bothers you, you can select other options that guarantee checks to your heirs for at least a certain number of years if you or you and your spouse die shortly after you retire. These are known as **life with five-year (or 10- or 20-year) certain** contracts. Even with these contracts, however, once the insurer has fulfilled its obligations it keeps whatever money is left. As a result, an annuity should not be your first choice if it's important to you to create a college fund for your grandkids or to leave a big bequest to your alma mater.

If your company doesn't offer to annuitize your 401(k), don't worry. There's nothing to prevent you from taking a lump-sum payout and buying a contract yourself. To do that, simply roll over your 401(k) money into an IRA with an insurance company and buy what is known as an **immediate** annuity. In an IRA annuity, you no longer have to get a spousal waiver to select a payout option other than joint-and-survivor. It may make sense to choose an option with bigger monthly checks if, say, your spouse has a pension of his or her own.

The chief attraction of an annuity is peace of mind. You don't have to worry about managing your money in your waning years. You can't blow your life's savings on a sour investment, and although your monthly checks are included in your taxable income, they won't trigger the five-alarm tax bills that an improperly handled lump-sum payout might. Finally and perhaps most important: With an annuity, you don't have to worry that your money will give out before you do. Even if you live well past your life expectancy, the insurer is obliged to keep cutting checks until you drop.

What you lose, however, is the chance to defend your

income against inflation. A 4% annual rise in consumer prices, for example, would halve the purchasing power of a fixed annuity check in about 18 years. If you took the money in a lump sum and invested it intelligently (we'll discuss how later on in the chapter), you should be able to make your money grow fast enough to keep you ahead of inflation.

Should You Take the Money in Installments?

Instead of (or as an alternative to) an annuity, your company may let you keep the money in your 401(k) and have it sent to you piecemeal, in installments. Depending on how your plan is designed, the installment option can range from being nearly as predictable as an annuity to being nearly as flexible as a lump-sum payout.

In the most basic installment plan, for example, your company may agree to pay you, say, $1,000 a month until either the money in your 401(k) gives out or you do. If you go first, the balance goes to your beneficiaries. In a restrictive plan, you might not be allowed to change your monthly installment once you start receiving payments, and you may even have to keep all your money in just one 401(k) fund, typically one of the capital preservation choices.

At the other end of the spectrum are plans that let you continue to direct your own 401(k) investments and withdraw money at will, essentially letting you use the plan as an IRA—without typical IRA fees. Assuming you are comfortable with the plan's investment options, this alternative has a lot to recommend it. One potential drawback: Your ability to get at your money will remain subject to the plan's disbursement machinery, which may be rather creaky. So before you sign on, make sure you understand

COMPARING YOUR OPTIONS AT RETIREMENT

Withdrawal Option	Must Employer Allow?	Advantages	Disadvantages
Direct rollover to IRA	Yes	• You gain full control of your investments. • You continue to get the benefits of tax-deferred growth until you withdraw the money.	• Taxes on withdrawals will be assessed at your top tax rate. • Income averaging not allowed.
Leave the money in the 401(k)	No	• You continue to direct investments, subject to the rules of the plan. • You continue to get the benefits of tax-deferred growth until you withdraw the money. • Income averaging remains an option.	• Your investment choices are limited to those offered by the 401(k) plan. • Your access to your cash may be restricted by the plan's administrative rules.
Annuitize	No	• You can't outlive your money. • You don't have to worry about investing your nest egg.	• The value of fixed annuity payments will be eroded by inflation. • If you die soon after annuitizing, the insurer may keep your money.
Installment withdrawals from your 401(k)	No	• You get a regular stream of income payments, without surrendering as much control as you would with an annuity. • If you die before your money is exhausted, your beneficiaries get the balance.	• Your investment choices and freedom to change the terms of your payments may be limited. • Depending on your plan's installment options, you may still outlive your money.
Five-year averaging (expires after 1999)	Yes	• You get access to all your money at a sharply reduced tax rate.	• Qualification rules are strict. • You must withdraw all your money from all plans of a similar type in one calendar year. • You can select this option only once.
Ten-year averaging	Yes	• You may save even more money than with five-year averaging.	• All five-year averaging restrictions apply, plus you must have been born before 1936.

how often you can request withdrawals and how long it will take to get the money.

Other plans offer installment arrangements that closely resemble annuities. For example, the company may agree to pay you equal monthly checks designed to empty your 401(k) over your predicted life span. In a refinement designed to keep you from going broke if you live longer than you are supposed to, the plan might recalculate your life expectancy—and the amount of your withdrawal—each year.

Installment plans have their own built-in drawbacks, including possible restrictions on how you can invest your money and whether you can change your mind once the installments start. Even if the plan allows you to direct your own investments, you will still be stuck with your 401(k)'s investment menu. Also, if you take a piecemeal payment from your plan and don't withdraw the remaining lump in the same calendar year, you've forever blown the chance to use **income averaging** to lower your tax bill should you later need to get at your money all at once. We'll explain income averaging later in this chapter.

Should You Take Your Money in a Lump Sum?

The first problem you have to deal with if you withdraw your 401(k) balance all at once is slipping that mound of money past Uncle Sam without losing most of it to taxes. Adding a five- or six-figure 401(k) payout to your other income would almost certainly push you into nosebleed tax territory. In 1998 you have to donate to Uncle Sam 36% of every dollar you made in excess of about $155,000 of taxable income. (That's if you're married and filing taxes jointly with your spouse. The 36% bracket starts at around $128,000 if you're single.) The haircut jumps to 39.6% on every dollar over 278,000 or so. If you figure in state taxes, the tax cost of removing your money from your 401(k) all at once could easily chop your retirement nest egg by 40% to 45%. That could be a lot of dutiful saving and smart investing down the drain.

Fortunately the tax code provides two major relief clauses for workers retiring with plump 401(k)s. First, you can postpone the tax reckoning by rolling your money over into an IRA. The process at retirement is exactly the same as described in the previous chapter for rolling money over when you change jobs. To avoid running afoul of the 20% withholding tax, you will need to set up an IRA account with your bank, brokerage, mutual fund company, or insurer and have your company send the money directly there. Once invested in an IRA, your money continues to grow tax-deferred, just as it did in your 401(k). Taxes don't enter the picture until you start pulling money out of the IRA. When you do, however, you'll have to take your tax medicine at full strength.

Your other choice is to pay your taxes right away and get it over with, but to do so according to a peculiar but highly favorable tax treatment called **five-year averaging**. (It's available only to employees retiring with money from a 401(k) or other work-related retirement plan before the year 2000; you can't average when you pull money out of an IRA.) Five-year averaging allows you to create two amiable fictions about your 401(k) distribution and calculate the tax on your payout accordingly. The fictions: that you received the money spread over five years instead of all at once, and that the payout was the only income you received that year. If you were born before January 1, 1936, you can select an even more generous tax break, known as **10-year averaging.**

HOW INCOME AVERAGING
SAVES YOU TAXES

Size of Lump-sum Distribution	Tax Liability on a Lump-sum Distribution under These Tax Options		
	Take Five-Year Averaging	Take 10-Year Averaging	Do Nothing and Pay Ordinary Income Tax
$100,000	$15,000	$14,470	$27,304
200,000	41,215	36,920	62,554
300,000	69,950	66,330	101,254
400,000	100,950	102,600	140,854
500,000	131,950	143,680	170,554

Assumptions: The taxpayer is married, files jointly with spouse, and has taxable income of $25,000 in addition to the retirement distribution.

In either case you still pay the total tax in the year you get the payout, but because of the hypothetical way you figure your taxes, you keep far more of it than if it were taxed like the rest of your income.

Suppose, for example, that you take your entire 401(k) balance of $200,000 out of your plan in a single year. If you have other taxable income of $25,000, your federal income tax alone on that sum would come to more than $62,000. With five-year averaging, it comes to just $41,200—an effective tax rate of just 20.6%. If you qualify for 10-year averaging, you can cut your tax rate even further, to just 18.5%.

One caution: Ten-year averaging doesn't always yield a lower tax bill because it requires you to figure your taxes based on tax rates that were in effect in 1986, when the top tax bracket was 50%. Generally speaking, 10-year averaging works out better when your lump sum is under $375,000. But individual cases can vary, so be sure to have your tax adviser calculate your tax bill both ways.

Needless to say, Uncle Sam closely guards averaging privileges. To qualify for it, you must take *all* the money out of your 401(k) and all similar employer-sponsored plans in the same year. (That's why if you pull money out on an installment plan, you can't change your mind after the first year and choose averaging for what's left.) You must have also have reached age 59½ and have participated in the plan for more than five years. Finally, you must not have used averaging in the past. It is truly a once-in-a-lifetime tax break.

Roll It Over or Average It?

Until averaging is repealed in 2000, this will remain the $64,000 question for lump sum payees (it's actually worth much more than that to most of them). The answer depends on the size or your payout, when you'll need the money and the rate of your return you can expect to earn on your retirement investments. The general rule is: if you plan to spend the money right away—say, to start a business or build yourself a retirement dream house on some windswept island—you should take averaging. If you can afford to leave the money untouched for three more years, then you're better off rolling it over (or keeping it in your 401(k), if your plan permits). The reason: eventually the benefits of continued tax-deferred growth outweigh the tax savings you get from averaging. However, many factors can tip the balance, so the only way to know for sure is to hire a financial adviser to create a retirement scenario and run the numbers for you.

In Case It's Not Yet Complicated Enough . . .

There is one other tax concern that you and your adviser need to keep in mind in planning your 401(k)'s endgame: the **minimum distribution** rule. It requires you to begin drawing down money in your tax-deferred accounts—including any money still in your 401(k), as well as any IRAs or other retirement plans—by April 1 of the year after you turn 70½. The IRS determines the minimum amount you have to take out based on your life expectancy or the joint life expectancy of you and a beneficiary.

Here's an example. The IRS says that your life expectancy is 16 years at age 70, so if you begin withdrawals at 70 you must withdraw one-sixteenth of your money. At the same time, you will have to decide how you plan to take distributions over the next 16 years. You can either continue to withdraw the same amount until your account is exhausted—and risk running out of money if you live longer than the IRS expects—or you can recalculate your life expectancy each year thereafter. With the **recalculation** option, you refigure your life expectancy and minimum withdrawal in each subsequent year. At 71, for example, your life expectancy has shrunk to 15.3 years, according to the IRS, and so that year you must withdraw 6.5% of your money (one divided by 15.3). If you don't take out enough, the tax penalty is a very painful 50% of the difference between what you should have pulled out and what you did.

The rule exists because the IRS wants to be sure it eventually collects the taxes that the 401(k) let you defer all those years. (It's not an issue for annuitizers, since they're already withdrawing money on a schedule designed to bring their 401(k) balance down to zero over their life span.) You can lower the required payouts somewhat by designating a younger joint beneficiary, but the IRS is wise to this stratagem: co-beneficiaries cannot be 10 years younger than you.

If they are, it doesn't help. You must use the joint life expectancy tables that apply to you and someone 10 years your Junior anyway.

Obviously the time to consult your financial adviser about this problem is at least five years in advance, when there is still time to plan around it. Don't let this last-minute tax trap spoil a career's work of building a solid 401(k).

The Remarkable Roth

You could conceivably avoid this age 70½ samba by transferring your money into an IRA and then moving it from there to a Roth IRA, a new kind of retirement plan exempt from minimum distribution rule. But since you'd have to pay taxes on the conversion from the regular IRA to the Roth, you'd almost certainly end up paying more taxes by doing that than by prolonging your 401(k) distribution by one of the methods above.

That doesn't mean, however, that you should forget about the Roth, one of the few real measures of taxpayer relief buried in the Taxpayer Relief Act of 1997. A Roth is a great way to supplement your retirement savings once you've already maxed out on your 401(k). While you have to pay taxes on the money you contribute to a Roth, your withdrawals are entirely tax-free, as long as you've held the account for five years and you're over 59½. And that's a remarkable deal.

Investing in Retirement

The final coda to a chapter on properly reaping the rewards of your 401(k) is how to make sure that those rewards stay reaped. This is an investing question, not a tax question, but it's worrisome how many people get it wrong. Too many retirees have the misconception that the work of investing ends once they've taken a distribution from their 401(k). At that point, they figure, a retiree's single investment goal is to produce the maximum amount of income with minimal risk to principal. In other words, load up on bonds and capital preservation investments and then live off your interest.

It won't work—at least, not for long. Rather than thinking of retirement as the end point of your investing career, think of it as the beginning of a new phase that figures to last 20, 25, or even 30 years. Over that length of time inflation will be sawing away relentlessly at the real value of your portfolio and the income it throws off. To stay ahead of the buzzsaw you will have to continue to think like a growth investor. That means that some of the investment practices you might have thought you could safely check at retirement's doorstep still apply:

You still have to save. If your retirement funds are to keep growing, you can't spend all the income your portfolio throws off. You'll have to plow some of it back into your investments as a reserve against inflation. For example, if inflation is running 4% a year and your portfolio returns 8%, you'll have to reinvest half of your return just to stay even after inflation.

This is especially important to remember if you annuitize. Unless you have plenty of outside investments that you are continuing to invest for growth, annuitizing your 401(k) means that most of your investment return will arrive at your mailbox in the form of monthly checks. The natural impulse is to treat them as spendable income. Don't—or you will begin to lose ground to inflation immediately. Instead, figure out what you need to spend and reinvest the rest, so that in a few years you can bring on another source of retirement income to meet the extra need created by inflation.

You still have to invest in stocks. You may have looked forward as much to retiring from the stock market's volatility as from your boss's volatile moods. Forget it: you still need the high returns that only the stock market can provide. The chart on page 193 shows you how important those returns are. If you can increase your real, after-inflation return from 2% (or about what bonds have paid in the long run) to 6% (the long-term record for stocks), you can make your money last an extra two decades or even longer.

Thus, in the early stages of your retirement you should think of yourself as still largely a growth investor—because you are. You have to be prepared to keep your income rising for a matter of decades, not years. Not only do you need the higher returns that you get from a large commitment from stocks, you still have the time to ride out downturns in the market.

Even when you get deeper into retirement, when safety of principal becomes a more important goal than future growth, you should not abandon stocks entirely. For example, in the sample late retirement portfolio shown on page 194, stocks should still account for 20% of your holdings.

You can spend capital: in fact, you will probably have to. When your parents were planning for their future, everyone knew that touching your principal in retirement was taboo. Perhaps that made a certain amount of sense in the preinflation era, when it was less risky to invest entirely in bonds and spend all your income: at least it forced retirees to limit their spending to their investment income. These days, however, that's not really possible, especially if you retain a large commitment to stocks, which don't throw

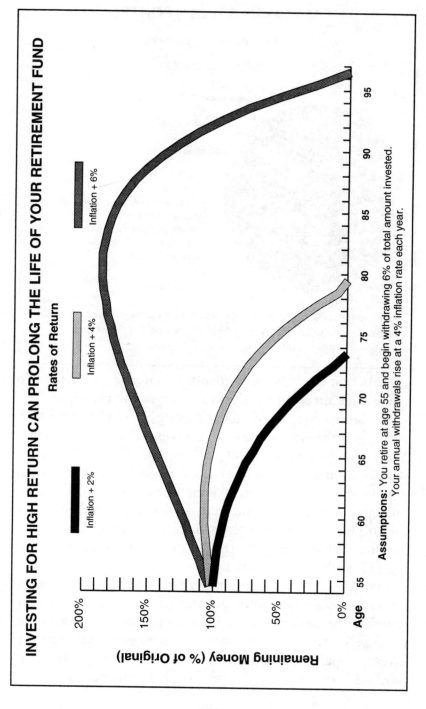

INVESTING FOR HIGH RETURN CAN PROLONG THE LIFE OF YOUR RETIREMENT FUND

Rates of Return

Inflation + 2%

Inflation + 4%

Inflation + 6%

Remaining Money (% of Original)

200%

150%

100%

50%

0%

Age 55 60 65 70 75 80 85 90 95

Assumptions: You retire at age 55 and begin withdrawing 6% of total amount invested. Your annual withdrawals rise at a 4% inflation rate each year.

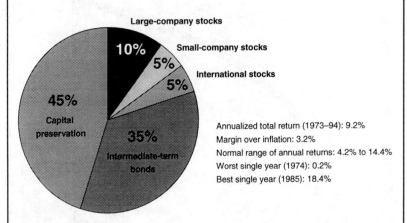

THE MAXIMUM SAFETY PORTFOLIO

(For late in retirement)

FIVE-FUND PORTFOLIO

Large-company stocks

10%

Small-company stocks

5%

International stocks

5%

45%

Capital
preservation

35%

Intermediate-term
bonds

Annualized total return (1973–94): 9.2%
Margin over inflation: 3.2%
Normal range of annual returns: 4.2% to 14.4%
Worst single year (1974): 0.2%
Best single year (1985): 18.4%

Assumptions: Portfolio is reset to desired ratios at the beginning of each year.
Sources: Individual Asset Planning Corp., Morristown. N.J.; Ibbotson &
Associates, SBBI 1994 Yearbook; Dimensional Fund Advisors.

off much in the way of dividends or interest payments. To make ends meet you will have to sell some principal.

While that may sound like advising you to eat your seed corn, it isn't—as long as your investments are growing. Your returns in retirement will consist of capital gains as well as dividends and interest income, just as they did when you were working. But as long as you spend only what you need and reinvest the rest, it doesn't matter whether the money you spend comes from capital appreciation or income. What really matters is that your total return be high enough to keep you ahead of inflation.

The fact is, when you start writing checks to cover your living expenses in your golden years, it won't matter whether the money comes from interest or capital gains or principal—or, for that matter, whether you acquired it by investing passively in index funds or by making brilliant fund selections in your 401(k). All that will really matter is whether there's enough money in your account to buy the quality of life you want. If you have managed your 401(k) wisely, you won't have to worry. The money will be there.

KEY POINTS

- Deciding how to take cash out of your 401(k) is one of the most complicated personal financial decisions you'll ever have to make. Start talking to a financial adviser at least five years before the decision is due.
- Taking your 401(k) payout in the form of an insurance company annuity leaves the investing worries to someone else and assures that you can't outlive your money. But since monthly annuity payments are fixed over your lifetime, their value is certain to be eroded by inflation.
- Your company may allow you to take money out of your plan in installments. Possible arrangements vary from a fixed monthly check to the freedom to withdraw money at will.
- Taking a lump-sum distribution allows you to retain control of your money and to invest it as you need to in retirement. To avoid a crippling tax bill, however, you should either roll over the money directly into an IRA or elect the special onetime tax treatment known as five- or 10-year averaging.
- Generally speaking, averaging makes more sense if you plan to spend all the money soon; a rollover works out best if you can afford to let the money grow undisturbed for three to five more years.
- Remember that in retirement you will have to invest your money as skillfully and almost as aggressively as you did before retirement. To counteract the depredations of inflation, you should always have some money in stocks.

INDEX

196

INDEX

INDEX